Tears at the Altar, Lament in My Breasts

Tears at the Altar, Lament in My Breasts

This Pastor Confronts Grief from the Pulpit

Andrea Campbell Byer Thomas

WIPF & STOCK · Eugene, Oregon

TEARS AT THE ALTAR, LAMENT IN MY BREASTS
This Pastor Confronts Grief from the Pulpit

Copyright © 2025 Andrea Campbell Byer Thomas. All rights reserved. Except for brief quotations in critical publications or reviews, no part of this book may be reproduced in any manner without prior written permission from the publisher. Write: Permissions, Wipf and Stock Publishers, 199 W. 8th Ave., Suite 3, Eugene, OR 97401.

Wipf & Stock
An Imprint of Wipf and Stock Publishers
199 W. 8th Ave., Suite 3
Eugene, OR 97401

www.wipfandstock.com

PAPERBACK ISBN: 979-8-3852-3852-1
HARDCOVER ISBN: 979-8-3852-3853-8
EBOOK ISBN: 979-8-3852-3854-5

VERSION NUMBER 04/14/25

Unless otherwise noted, Scripture quotations are from New Revised Standard Version Bible, copyright © 1989 National Council of the Churches of Christ in the United States of America. Used by permission. All rights reserved worldwide.

Where noted, Scripture quotations are from Holy Bible, New International Version®, NIV® Copyright ©1973, 1978, 1984, 2011 by Biblica, Inc.® Used by permission. All rights reserved worldwide.

To my *Fantastic Four*—

Arleigh Hartfield Byer II, my second-born, who now regales the heavens with his wit and wisdom,

Arleigha, Arleigh-Ann, and Arleigho, who carry the light and laughter of our shared journey forward.

This book is for you, my loves, for teaching me the depths of grief and the unyielding power of love.

For showing me resilience in the face of heartbreak, and for reminding me, always, that life's most sacred work is to hold on to each other—even in the storm.

To the one whose absence carves a presence in every word of this book and to the ones whose presence heals what was broken,

You are my *Fantastic Four*.

With every breath, with every beat, with every page—

I love you fiercely. Always.

For a long time I have held my peace,
I have kept still and restrained myself;
now I will cry out like a woman in labor,
I will gasp and pant.

—Isaiah 42:14

If grief is the price we pay for love,
lament is the song we sing
when love has been shattered.

—Andrea's reflection

Contents

Preface | ix
Acknowledgments | xi
Introduction | xiii

Arleigh's Eulogy | 1
Lament Without An Amen | 5

Part 1
Remembering What I Cannot Forget: Personal Stories | 7

Part 2
Bible Talk | 73

Part 3
Reflection and Guidance | 197

Bibliography | 217

Preface

THIS BOOK EMERGES FROM the deepest places of my soul, carved out by the sharp edges of grief and the tender hands of love. It is not just a collection of thoughts; it is a testimony to the journey of lament, a spiritual practice that the church has often avoided but desperately needs to reclaim. It is a journey I never imagined I would take, one that began with the loss of my son, Arleigh, and unfolded into an exploration of the spaces where sorrow and faith collide.

As a pastor, I have walked alongside people in their darkest hours, offering words of comfort and prayers of hope. Yet, when grief found me, it spoke a language I had never fully understood—a language of silence and screams, of breathless cries and whispered prayers. In those moments, I found that the church, which had been my sanctuary, often struggled to hold space for the rawness of pain. Instead, it rushed to resolve, to praise, to sanitize. But grief does not need resolution; it needs recognition. Lament does not require answers; it demands acknowledgment.

This book is written for those who have ever wept by the rivers of Babylon, wondering how to sing the Lord's song in a strange land. It is for the church that must learn to sit in the ashes with the grieving, to hold sacred space for lament, and to create liturgies that honor the full spectrum of human emotion. It is for pastors who must learn to balance the call to preach good news with the responsibility to name and mourn the brokenness of the world. It is for anyone who has ever dared to wrestle with God and love God at the same time.

You will find in these pages a raw honesty about my own journey, woven together with the ancient cries of Scripture, theological reflections, and practical insights for the church. You will hear the echoes of my son's laughter and the depth of my family's sorrow. You will encounter stories of displacement, injustice, and resilience that call us to examine our collective response to trauma and loss.

This is not a book that will tie your grief into a neat bow or offer platitudes in the face of pain. It is an invitation to wrestle, to question, to lament, and ultimately, to find hope—not in the absence of grief but in the presence of God who meets us there.

To those who have loved deeply and lost profoundly, this book is for you. May it remind you that your tears are sacred, your cries are heard, and your lament is holy. May it call the church to a deeper understanding of its role in holding space for the wounded and the weary. And may it inspire us all to sing songs of lament that make room for healing and hope.

This is my lament. This is my offering. This is my testimony.

Acknowledgments

THIS BOOK IS THE culmination of love, loss, and the steadfast presence of so many who have walked with me through the valleys and stood with me on the mountaintops. It would not exist without the unwavering support, encouragement, and prayers of an extraordinary community of people.

To my beloved Fantastic Four—my children, my heartbeats, my life—you are the reason I rise each day. Thank you for your courage, for your love, and for walking this road with me. You are my strength and my joy. I love you to life!

To my "honban" Jerry. Thank you for having the balls to stay in the bleak and in the warmth. I love you.

To my sister-like cousin, Darlene Charles, in whom I have seen Jesus. Thank you for understanding, and for offering your shoulder without hesitation.

To my covenant sisters and other clergy siblings, who showed up, held my hand, cleaned my floors, watered my plants, simply sat with me, helped me plan a memorial service, laughed and let me cry, cuss, and carry on—your acts of compassion were sermons in themselves. You carried me when I could not carry myself, and for that, I am forever grateful.

To Dr. Teresa Fry-Brown, who tagged me "a dangerous preacher" and commanded, "Write the books, Black Woman," thank you for seeing me, for believing in me, and for challenging me to step boldly into my calling.

ACKNOWLEDGMENTS

To my friends and my family—biological and chosen—you booked flights, you drove for hours, you came. Hand to heart, thank you for your support when life first became shitty, and for creating space for my grief beyond the immediate moment.

To the COVID Conquering Cohort of Class 2022, I love you guys.

To Dr. Joel Kemp, advisor extraordinaire, for holding my tears as sacred and my story as warranted. You will remain.

To Arleigh's friends, who sat with me, shared laughter through tears, and reminded me of the joy my son brought to the world, thank you for giving me your pieces of him to hold onto. Your stories have become part of his legacy and part of my becoming.

To God, who breathes life into lament and hope into despair, thank you for meeting me in the depths of my grief and carrying me. It hurts like hell, and you are still here. This book is a sacred offering to you and to the church you call to embody your love.

To everyone who has shared this journey with me, you are part of this story. Thank you for walking alongside me. May this book honor your kindness and reflect the power of love and community to transform even the deepest pain.

Introduction

> "I am feeding a child who is no longer being sustained by my milk. My breasts are swollen with the pain of absence. My womb is throbbing with its attempts to adjust. I am missing my child. Can you feel that, Lord?"
> (Journal excerpt)

THERE'S AN OLD SAYING, "Time heals all wounds," but it is an open-ended lie. Not all wounds heal over time. Some wounds remain, changing shape but never disappearing, coloring every corner of life with their weight. As an immigrant woman of color learning to sing the Lord's song in this strange land called surviving the death of a child, I offer this work. My goal is to help us collectively reclaim the value of lament in our worship life—as a tool of liberation and healing.

In these pages, I weave together the stories of my own grief, the laments of Scripture, and the voices of those who have shared their pain with me. I explore what it means to be a pastor who grieves, a mother who mourns, and a believer who questions. I wrestle with the ways the church has often failed to meet people in their suffering and offer practical steps for creating communities of care and compassion.

This book arises from a wilderness no one chooses. It is a land of grief and loss that many of us are forced to navigate. It is

INTRODUCTION

an offering, born out of raw pain and deep love, for those who are searching for language to express what often feels unspeakable. It is an invitation to wrestle with the tension between faith and sorrow, to lean into lament as a means of liberation and healing, and to reimagine worship as a space where all emotions—joy and despair, hope and rage—are not only welcomed but necessary.

In reflecting on how we respond to grief, I am reminded of a moment when President Barack Obama posted about the death of his family's dog, Bo. The outpouring of condolences and sorrow from thousands of people on social media was striking. Bo was a dog—a beloved member of their family, yes—but a dog nonetheless. I marvel at the depth of concern and empathy shown for the death of a pet. If the death of a dog warrants such care, how much more should we express concern for the deaths of human beings? How much more should we make space for the complex layers of grief in our communities and our worship? And yet, we often fail to do so.

Unfortunately, many interpreters of the Bible have chosen to tone down the reality of ever-present trauma in the human experience. This omission has led to worship practices that center on positivity, prematurely skipping to the resurrection without sitting at the cross or in the tomb. Such practices neglect the deep, nuanced hardships of life. In response, this work seeks to encourage us to lean into lament as an essential practice of faith. By normalizing lament, we resist the overwhelming forces of despair that threaten to drown us, much like the waters of Babylon that the psalmist speaks of in Ps 137.

This is not a book about "getting over" grief or providing easy answers to the hard questions of life. It is not even a book that offers a linear way to think about grief. It is a book about sitting with the questions and allowing ourselves to feel the weight of our pain while seeking liberation through the practice of lament. It is a call to churches and communities to acknowledge the reality of human suffering, to make room for lament in our liturgies, sermons, and worship practices, and to recognize lament as a form of resistance against systems that perpetuate harm.

INTRODUCTION

Moreover, this book is about liberation from the silence and suppression that often accompany grief and trauma. Lament allows us to name our pain, to confront it, and to offer it to God without fear. It is a tool for dismantling the toxic positivity that demands we "be strong" or "move on" without fully processing our experiences. It is a way of reclaiming our humanity and affirming that all of who we are, even our brokenness, is welcomed by God.

This book is for those who have experienced loss, for those who love someone who is grieving, and for those who seek to be the hands and feet of God in a world that so often breaks our hearts. It is for the mother who weeps for her child, the pastor who struggles to reconcile faith with sorrow, the friend who wants to help but doesn't know how, and the community leader who longs to create spaces of healing and hope.

In these pages, I invite you to journey with me through Scripture, where lament is not only present but central. We will explore passages that challenge us to see God as an active presence in our suffering. And we will look at how lament can be a prophetic act, calling us to engage with the injustices of the world and to advocate for equity and healing.

This work is eclectic, weaving together personal narrative, biblical reflection, and practical tools for ministry. It is an offering to those who grieve, to those who minister to the grieving, and to those who long to create spaces where the fullness of human experience can be brought before God. May these pages remind us all that lament is a bold declaration of trust in a God who hears, sees, and sits with us in our pain.

May we remember Zion together. May we sing, weep, and wrestle. And may we be liberated through the work of lament.

Arleigh's Eulogy

IT WAS A HOT summer in Bronx, New York. Yet, none of that mattered on the morning of August 30, 1995, when Arleigh Hartfield Byer II was born to Andrea and Arleigh Byer. The day quickly turned from just hot and miserable to super-charged and excited! Arleigh had arrived!

From the moment he took his first breath here, Arleigh had an appetite that was comparable only to that of his older sister, which he eventually surpassed. The boy could eat! He went from "May I have some more please?" as a little boy to "Are you going to finish that?" as an adult.

Arleigh was multi-talented. He sketched. He played the steel pan, recorder, trumpet, keyboard, and a little bit of guitar. He modeled and owned the runway. He was fluent in Spanish. He taught himself auto-mechanics and maintained his car himself. He built stuff. When he was seven years old, he built a plane. The body was made of craft sticks and the engine was made of parts he took from his mother's appliances. He was determined to make the plane fly, and he did! He was a happy child who loved the outdoors and all the adventures that came with that. He loved talking about growing up in Antigua, climbing trees and eating.

He loved his family, and his family loved him. Yet, for all the good qualities Arleigh had, his mother is convinced that something was missing because this boy wasn't really into calypso and soca. That's unheard of for a child belonging to Andrea! What? He liked rap music and offered a well-thought-out defense of Kanye West (before Kanye's nonsense days). What was the point of spending all that time toning in the gym, if he wasn't going to soca?

Arleigh was not afraid or ashamed to engage in manual labor. He spent an entire summer learning fire sprinkler work from his stepdad, Jerry—(really, the dad who stepped up.) As a teacher, he was fiercely protective of "his kids" as he called them. He was passionate about youth empowerment and challenging the cultural norm of injustice. Although he loved red and black and wore them proudly, he was unafraid to wear pink as part of his contribution to the fight against breast cancer.

He was brave. While he was a student at Northeast High, he participated in Adimu Men of Excellence and the marching band at Blanche Ely High School. Arleigh was funny. When he participated in the Christmas plays at Village UMC, it was usually in multiple roles, and each role would be played with a different accent and persona. The man was gifted!

Anyone who ever truly engaged him quickly understood the futility of arguing with him. There was no winning an argument with Arleigh Byer II. He also had the uncanny ability to make you do introspective work. Like his mother and siblings, Arleigh-Ann, Arleigha, and Arleigho, Arleigh was an avid reader, and he read widely. He was not afraid to ask the harder questions of any text, including the biblical text. He and his mother would have theological conversations around doctrine and practice and often did book studies together. These were great bonding times for them both.

He graduated from Northeast High School, then Florida A&M University and just knew that he was going to be an attorney. His mother would tell him to keep his heart open because "you never know what God might do with your mind and mouth." This would make him erupt into laughter. That laughter. Have you ever heard Arleigh laugh? I mean, have you ever heard Arleigh really laugh? That sound could be heard from clear across the way and would evoke laughter out of you even if the sound of his laughter may have just woken you from a deep sleep. His laughter was the sound of sheer joy, and it was contagious.

Arleigh had the LSAT in the bag toward his journey to becoming an attorney. He was excited about that. He was focused. He spent hours in the library continuing late into the night. Then he would eat every edible thing in the house.

On August 24, 2019, Arleigh Hartfield Byer II exhaled for the last time here on earth. We miss him deeply. We miss him daily. Certainly, the great hereafter must be full of Arleigh's loud, ringing laughter. If heaven is what they say, thank God, there is more than enough food there.

Lament Without An Amen

> Out of the depths I cry to you O Lord ... (Psalm 130:1)
>
> If I go forward, God is not there; or backward, I cannot perceive him; on the left God hides, and I cannot behold God; I turn to the right, but God is nowhere in sight. (Job 23:8–9)

As a Black Caribbean woman living in the US, my life has been marked by various crises. In the Caribbean, certain interpretations of the Bible often held more weight than the teachings and examples of Jesus himself. When my mother died at the age of forty-three, leaving me and my grandmother to care for my five siblings, two of whom have developmental challenges, I was met with a common response: "Don't question God." When my youngest sibling, just five years old when our mother died, began showing signs of emotional distress, and I searched the entire island for help, the prevailing sentiment was "You just need to have faith." But the undeniable truth is that faith does not prevent life's hardships. Unfortunately, neither the church nor society seemed to grasp this reality.

I choose to confront my trauma because pretending that pain isn't painful does not make it hurt any less. I stand alongside Job, and I stand with Mrs. Job. Her lamentation is a raw expression of honesty, and I do not hush her. Instead, I join her in expressing the depth of her distrust, her wounds, and her grief. While I cannot fully comprehend the extent of her suffering since I am not her, and have no desire to be her, I lament alongside her from my own place of unspeakable pain. I can only wonder (not imagine) how she managed to endure. Mrs. Job, how did you find the strength to carry on after such heart-wrenching events?

I resonate with the sense of futility described by the writer of Ecclesiastes. It often feels as if everything is in vain. Since becoming a mother, not a day has passed without my fervent prayers for the well-being of my children. I have knelt in prayer with other mothers, all of us united by the hope that our children will navigate life's challenges, dream big, and live those dreams, protected and guided by God. Since the death of Arleigh, there have been moments when I have struggled to find a reason to celebrate, echoing the words of the despondent preacher: "All is vanity." I wonder, Preacher, how did you climb out of that deep abyss?

I empathize with Mary and Martha during the agonizing interval between their brother's death and the miracle of his resurrection. The frustration over Jesus' apparent delay courses through me, sending shivers down my spine. Questions about Jesus' absence during my own moments of desperate waiting for a different outcome fill my conversations with him. Jesus, if you had been there, my son would not have died. Where were you, Jesus, when I sat there hoping for a different report?

I stand beside Mary, the mother of Jesus, and my heart aches in unison with hers. My maternal instinct longs to comfort her, yet I find myself at a loss. So, I rock back and forth with her, letting the suppressed scream within me build momentum deep in my core. Death is a painful sting. All I can offer Mary is a heartfelt, "Dear Mary . . ." Today, my tears are especially salty as I cry not only for myself but also for you and the countless other mothers whose shared language is the raw, tearful form of expression known as weeping. Dear Mary, have you slept since?

Part 1

Remembering What I Cannot Forget: Personal Stories

Chapter 1

No one ever told me that grief was so much like fear.
—C. S. Lewis, A Grief Observed

Mammy: Norma Georgiana Cecelia Bowers Lake

I WAS JUST TWENTY-THREE years old, a young mother and wife, when the tragic event happened: my mother's death at the tender age of forty-three. Three years prior to her death, I was told that she had a stroke which occurred during a surgery to remove a brain tumor. The contrast was stark; my mother entered the operating room as a vibrant, physically active woman with a contagious smile and legendary gardening skills, and she emerged, tragically, with her left side paralyzed, drastically altering her mobility. This abrupt transformation was the prelude to a huge shift in my own life.

In the aftermath of the surgery, my mother's once-active life became a stationary existence, tethered to her bed, and marked by brokenness. I, as the eldest, along with my grandmother, assumed the role of caregivers to my younger siblings, among whom were two with developmental challenges that remained undiagnosed, though obvious. My mother had cared for them well, up until she herself needed to be cared for.

My mother had an extraordinary talent for impersonation that could have earned her a spot in Hollywood overnight. Her mimicry was so spot-on that gossiping was a futile endeavor, as you would immediately recognize who she was imitating. She was gentle to a fault, often allowing people to get away with more than they should have. She constantly shifted her own boundaries to appease those around her. In her pursuit of acceptance, she donned various masks, hiding her true self.

By molding herself into what others desired, she chose to silence her own dreams and aspirations out of fear of rejection. She refrained from celebrating my achievements publicly to avoid potential criticism. This pattern of self-editing eventually eroded her authentic voice. Although I was still young throughout her life, I observed her transformation closely, and her behaviors began to influence me. Like her, I too often plastered on a smile in response to condescending remarks, all for the sake of maintaining peace. However, I have come to realize that this form of peace is superficial, fleeting, and ultimately unfulfilling.

My mother's father was not the kindest to her. Others in her life were no better, frequently promising to compensate her for her work or for the plants they acquired from her but never following through. These unpaid debts only came to light when, on rare occasions, one of these debtors casually acknowledged their overdue obligations. My mother would graciously smile and reply with an accommodating "okay." This folly frustrated me deeply, just as it frustrates me and my children whenever I do the same thing. However, my mother was not the stereotypical "hurt people hurt people" case study; she did not function to make others feel inferior. Instead, she coped by suppressing her pain, adopting an attitude of forgiveness, and only revealing her true hurt in private, in tears.

Mammy, as we affectionately called her, was my first teacher. She taught me to read when I was three years old. I still remember coming home from Sunday School, eating and sitting on her lap while she taught me to read from "Naaman and the Little Maid" based on 2 Kings 5.

PART 1: PERSONAL STORIES

She taught me poetry, and held my hand and taught me to shape letters. Mammy was creative and passed on her love of making to me. We had so much fun making all sorts of things! It was Mammy who introduced me to calypso. I loved it then, and I love it now! She took me to calypso shows with her, and during the Carnival season, she took my siblings and I to watch the parade of troops. Oh, what joy!

Her nephew, Alister, often recounts a moment from my infancy that remains vivid in his memory. He recalls that we were at the hospital when my mother, Mammy, was holding me in her arms. As she walked, she suddenly tripped, sending her into a series of falls, rolls, and flips across the ground. Watching in both horror and awe, Alister observed that despite the impact, Mammy never loosened her grip. When she finally came to a stop, her legs were scraped, and her elbows were bruised, but her hands remained raised, still clutching me tightly. "Your feet never touched the ground," he often says. "I can never forget. Aunt Norma meant that nothing was going to happen to you."

Mammy also had a loyal canine companion named Castro, who seemed to absorb her pain and fiercely guarded both her and the ICU section of her plant nursery. Many people disliked Castro, likely because he sensed their deviance toward Mammy and refused to tolerate it. And although Castro was also protective of me, I did not feel the same sense of liking toward him. My aversion to Castro stemmed from my general dislike of all dogs—most animals, really.

Throughout her life, my mother did not experience the joy of a birthday celebration or any form of commemoration of her existence, except the awards she got from our village for her plant nursery. Although she never verbalized her dissatisfaction, I'll never forget the night when I walked up on her quietly weeping under the moonlit sky in her usual spot out in the yard. When I inquired about her tears, she explained that earlier that day, she overheard when someone told me that I would never amount to anything good. I remember that afternoon as if it were yesterday. I was ten years old. I remember the anger that shook my little body and the confidence in my voice as I replied, "Watch and see." When Mammy revealed that she had overheard the comment, I was at a loss for how to respond. All I could do was touch her gently with my small hand and promise that I would indeed amount to something good. We both understood that it was a promise already fulfilled, as the signs were everywhere.

Chapter 2

ON OCCASION, MAMMY TOOK me with her to work on weekends when she was responsible for her employers' children during parties or social events. I remember those moments vividly. I also recall my distaste for the family, who exhibited a lack of basic courtesy. Who enters a room occupied by another person without greeting them and proceeds to demand breakfast? The nerve! The daughter of the household, older than me, was particularly rude, and I disliked her immensely. During these visits, I was tasked with helping her with her reading, which was atrocious—especially, in my opinion, for someone as disrespectful as she. While I was helping her, she often found reasons to belittle me, whether it was my accent, my hair, my skin, or my lack of fashionable clothing. One day, in an act of defiance, when she commented on my "coarse" hair, I retorted that my hair was crowning the same brain that was teaching her how to read. Predictably, she reported me for various infractions, all of which were fabricated except for the comment I had made. Her parents, in response to the reports, conveyed that if it weren't for my assistance to her, I wouldn't be allowed to return. While they scolded me, my "student" stood behind them facing me and making mocking faces at me. I wished they would fire my mother, so I wouldn't have to go back to their house.

When we got home from work that Sunday evening, it was evident that Mammy was troubled by the confrontation between me and her employers' daughter over the weekend. She appeared shaken, a far cry from her usual calm demeanor. When she finally addressed the situation, she surprised me with her affirmation of my assertion and self-defense. It was the first time she had defended either herself or me in any way. I remember feeling giggly.

Chapter 3

MAMMY CARRIED AN INTENSE emotional depth I couldn't reach with my limited understanding as a child. As I grew older and began to learn more about her life, I began to appreciate the extent of her pain. During her illness, while I sat at her bedside, I would inquire about her childhood. Initially, she attempted to evade my questions. However, as she realized I held no judgment or condemnation and that I was genuinely interested in her story, she became more open and began to share. Recounting less pleasant experiences, including forced sexual encounters, evoked visceral reactions in her: rapid, shallow breaths, a stiffened posture, a faraway look, and a deepened voice. I remained by her side throughout, weeping alongside her, and loving her unwaveringly. She understood that I valued her as a human being, and not just for the maternal favors she provided.

Approximately two weeks before her death, Mammy shared a heart-wrenching request. She insisted that when she died, I must assume responsibility for her children and keep the family together. My initial response was to suppress the thought and to reject the possibility. However, she wouldn't allow me to evade her request. She was resolute, expressing that her death was imminent, and she entrusted me with the care of my siblings. Like Peter, who contested Jesus' fate in Matt 16:22, I vehemently protested, telling her that she would not die, and she should stop saying such nonsense. That was, of course, my own fear and uncertainty making demands. About a week later, her condition deteriorated. She became lethargic, her appetite waned, and she ceased to eliminate waste regularly. It was later explained to me that her body was shutting down. The vivacious body that once climbed trees was gradually fading away.

One Saturday morning, three years after the surgery that had left her paralyzed, an ambulance transported Mammy to the hospital when she failed to wake up. Each day, I spent hours at her bedside still trying to wake her up. One day, hope sprang when she called my name. There was so much I wanted to say to her, but I did not feel comfortable saying any of it in the presence of someone who was visiting at that time. I only assured her of my presence and my love. The last time I heard her voice was when she lay there in the hospital calling my name.

The call from the hospital notifying me of her death was cold and abrupt, with the caller brusquely asking, "You know that your mother has died, right?" I remember a numbness engulfing me, followed by anger as I retorted, "How would I have known? Is this any way to inform someone of their mother's death? Do you have no heart?" And then, I wept. Yet, the full weight of Mammy's death would not truly register within me for many years, until another death occurred—one that continues to weigh heavily on my spirit to this day.

Chapter 4

When we lose someone we have loved deeply, we are left with a grief that can paralyze us emotionally. When they die, a part of us dies too.

—Henri Nouwen, *Bread for the Journey*

Granny—Frances Iola Lewis

When I entered my grandmother's kitchen, she was seated at her usual spot at the kitchen table, surrounded by some of her usual paraphernalia: a find-a-word puzzle book, her Bible, a writing pad, and a pen. I took a seat across from her, and our conversation flowed organically, one topic leading to another. The sounds of village life—barking dogs, bleating sheep, crowing roosters, parents calling to their children, neighbors cackling with each other—all went silent while we talked. Somewhere within this extensive exchange, a question I had harbored for a long time erupted from within me: "Granny, how do you manage it? How do you go on after losing two of your children?" Her response was simple yet insightful. "Mmmm. All I know is that I have to keep on living each day I'm given." It was as if, for the first time, she acknowledged the deaths of two of her children, one of whom was my mother. Tears began to stream down her face as she wailed, eventually plunging into some of the other burdens she carried.

My grandmother was a devout churchgoer, a daily reader of her Bible, a regular attendee of Bible studies and prayer meetings, a singer of hymns, and someone who prayed about every aspect of life, no matter how trivial. Despite this strong faith, she had never realized that she could verbalize her pains, let alone that the church had a rich tradition of lamenting such sorrows, both collectively and individually. She had been indoctrinated by her local religious community not to question God, dwell excessively on life's hardships, or express her grief openly. On the day of our conversation, my initial question seemed to liberate her from this prison of contradictory beliefs. She granted herself permission not only to acknowledge and name her pain but also to lament it. It was through this act of lament that true healing could finally begin.

Usually, my grandmother kept her sorrows tightly guarded, but on that day, her chest lost its capacity to contain them, and they poured out in torrents. She shared stories of her struggles and the abuses she endured, often using words from the Psalms and well-known hymns. Throughout her lamentations, the repeated phrases "O Lord" and "O God" punctuated her cries.

She needed to heal, although I'm not sure she fully comprehended how much she needed to undertake the work of grieving and lamenting. However, as I witnessed her unshackling expressions of pain and sorrow, it became evident to me. Sitting with her during this cathartic release was not uncomfortable, although it was undoubtedly painful to hear some of her accounts. After what felt like an eternity (though it was indeed hours later), she wiped her tears with the hem of her dress, blew her nose, and closed the chorus with another round of "O God."

For my grandmother, God, the church, and the Bible were central to her life, a trinity of sorts that deeply shaped her existence. I believe it was from her that I learned to approach hermeneutics the way that I do. While she may not have been called a theologian, her frequent musings like, "Well, Lord, I wonder what Jesus would say about that," always encouraged me to engage in theological contemplation. Unbeknownst to her, she nurtured my innate curiosity and guided this budding student of the Bible toward a path she would never live to witness.

Chapter 5

IN THE YEARS FOLLOWING her death, I often reflected on the moments we shared through conversation, silence, and life itself. One question lingered in my mind: Why, despite her wisdom and her penchant for seeking God's guidance, had I never heard her inquire of God about the deaths of her own children?

Billie Holiday once sang about the persistent presence of trauma in human life. Her song "Good Morning Heartache" contains advice from which many people could benefit. The Bible also provides numerous examples of the human need to pause, acknowledge, and heal from life's wounds and hardships.

There's no need to wait for anyone's permission to grieve, nor should we let others dictate how we should grieve. Grieving is often an essential path to healing. Those who haven't processed their pain often romanticize suffering, perhaps as a way to numb their own anguish, inadvertently causing harm to others. Grief doesn't equate to weakness; in fact, those who fully engage in their grieving process exhibit immense strength.

Shelly Rambo's book *Spirit and Trauma: A Theology of Remaining* brings attention to the experiences of Holy Saturday—the period between Jesus' crucifixion and his resurrection. If the crucifixion represents acute trauma, such as the death of a loved one, sexual violence, state violence, or the death of a child, then Holy Saturday, and even the empty tomb itself, symbolizes the challenging phase where one navigates life beyond a metaphorical death but cannot yet see a clear path forward. Trauma reshapes life and alters the way we perceive it. Although Scripture contains numerous accounts of trauma and pain, these stories often have seemingly happy endings, leading Bible readers and interpreters to overlook the Holy Saturdays within them, rushing instead to the Easter narratives.

However, neglecting Holy Saturday comes at our own peril. When her two children died, my grandmother's church attempted to hasten her journey from Good Friday to Easter, much like the church I served in when my own son died. I encountered statements like, "You're a pastor; you should move on," or "You should know better than to dwell in grief." However, the death of a child isn't something one simply gets over. I refused to allow myself to be hurried or silenced. Having observed the experiences of grief in my mother and grandmother, I understood the importance of Holy Saturday as a necessary bridge—a place to dwell for a while before Easter.

Traumatic events have a way of rupturing our hope, scattering fragments of our hearts to unexpected places. Grief itself is a form of trauma and cannot be resolved by reciting comforting clichés about God's plan or the need for another angel. Grief and lamentation are valuable gifts, providing the space and hope necessary for our lives to slowly mend. Addressing society's insensitive treatment of grief and lamentation, as well as redesigning our worship experiences, requires introspection and reevaluation. This critical assessment is essential to create the room needed for lamentation to be recognized as the vital healing bridge it truly is.

Chapter 6

IN THE EIGHTIES WHEN my grandmother retired, Antigua's retirement age was sixty, and that arrangement worked quite well for people with young children and jobs to go to who could use the wonderful and typically free babysitting services of grandmothers! For us, the extended family system was a way of life, and sometimes up to four generations lived in the same household. For my household, it was three generations: my grandmother, my mother, and us children. Granny was always a constant presence in my life.

Although she was supportive of my call to the ordained ministry and often prayed for me, Granny was the first one who told me that ministry was a dangerous road to walk. On several occasions, she quoted to me what I only much later came to realize was hymn 253 from *The Hymnal of the Evangelical United Brethren Church*: "Believe not those who say the upward path is smooth, lest you should stumble in the way and faint before the truth."[1] Whereas at first, I thought that Granny was a poet, I later learned that the words came from this hymn.

Her humming and la-la-la-ing were part of the soundtrack of my early youth into my adult years. I know all the words to many of the hymns of the faith not only because we sang them lustily on Sunday mornings, each morning at family prayer-time, at school morning prayers, but also because I heard Granny singing them

---

1. *Hymnal of The Evangelical United Brethren Church*, 253.

(mostly off-key) at home all the time. She was not a great singer, but she did sound better than Mammy did!

True to her African heritage, Granny also had many proverbs or sayings for life's issues. Whenever we children asked for something that was not in the home budget, she would remind us that we were "stones under water that did not know when the sun was hot." And with that, without arguing, we would go back to playing or whatever it was that we were up to. She was a strong believer in the ultimate vision of God for the world, and in the face of human cruelty, would intone, "Heaven will split the justice." This was her way of telling us that God will alleviate suffering and redeem the wronged. Oftentimes when she lamented hurt, this saying was a part of her offering. For Granny, the justice of God was synonymous with the absence of any kind of pain. Granny was loathe to participate in gossip or other forms of behavior that hurt people.

Chapter 7

One day, I overheard a conversation when a villager paid an impromptu visit to our home—a common practice in the community. The dialogue began innocuously, then soon turned to gossip. My grandmother immediately halted the conversation, admonishing the gossipmonger that she had chosen the wrong audience. When I later asked her about this, she sagely advised, "When someone brings gossip to you, send them away; you are likely next on their list. The same stick that beats the wild, beats the tame." Her wisdom reinforced my own dislike for invasive behavior. I also become uneasy when I observe people criticizing those with whom they seem friendly "behind their backs." In Antiguan parlance, we deem such individuals "dangerous."

My grandmother was an advocate for contentment and self-sufficiency. She often cautioned us against envy, stating, "What you lack, do without." She was resourceful and inventive, embodying the adage "Necessity makes water flow uphill." She also tended to not rock the societal boat too much and lived much within the confines of what society deemed "normal," including the way she dressed.

I remember sewing a romper for her, and my delight was immeasurable when she wore it publicly. It was a departure from her usual attire, and she took it as an opportunity to celebrate my craftsmanship. Unfortunately, there are no photographs of her in the outfit, as she was generally averse to being photographed. Despite this, she was exceedingly generous and welcoming, characteristics that perhaps stemmed from her own emotional complexities.

Our closeness was not devoid of challenges, including her occasional bouts of anger. She had set guidelines about our arrival time from school, and one day, I arrived a mere ten minutes late. The ensuing public reprimand was disproportionate to the minor tardiness. Years later, when we discussed the incident, she expressed regret for her actions. She admitted to times when her emotional vulnerabilities led to unwarranted outbursts. It was as if her fear for my potential failure was displaced onto me in a misguided attempt to protect me.

As we both matured, I found her increasingly open-minded, distinguishing her from many of her contemporaries. Although deeply rooted in her faith, she acknowledged that life's complexities could not be solely dictated by religious doctrine.

Chapter 8

The wound that never heals is the most sacred. Let it bleed.

—Yaa Gyasi, *Homegoing*

If you know someone who has lost a child, and you're afraid to mention them because you think you might make them sad by reminding them that they died, you're not reminding them. They didn't forget they died. What you're reminding them of is that you remembered that they lived, and that is a great, great gift.

—Elizabeth Edwards, *Resilience: Reflections on the Burdens and Gifts of Facing Life's Adversities*

Arleigh Hartfield Byer II—My Son

It doesn't even make any sense that my son's name is included in this kind of conversation. Why is this? How could it be that the God I am told is always in control seems to have lost control of the moment in question? Every day, I rage against this reality of my child's death that has my heart redefining what should be its organic schedule.

PART 1: PERSONAL STORIES

The eulogy I composed was nothing more than a truncated chronicle of his twenty-three years. Public rituals of mourning, with their artificial timelines, compress the enormity of a life into mere moments. I was disoriented—so much so that two weeks post his death, I hadn't even begun planning a memorial service. Traditional funerals hold no appeal for me; instead, a worship service honoring Arleigh's life was ultimately orchestrated at the suggestion of a fellow clergy colleague.

Queries about my well-being oscillated between searing pain and numbing grief, as though my emotional register could only alternate between two extremes. When asked, "How are you?" my visceral response was, "I am dying." Because in many ways, I was. One second, my heart felt like a torn cuticle, and the next second, it felt like my finger was being slammed between the door of a car. It was one, then the other, and it was a while before I understood that this was the new rhythm of my heart. I long for the day when the rhythms of my heart are no longer dictated by his absence but rather by the enduring love and pride I hold for my son, Arleigh Hartfield Byer II.

Arleigh Hartfield Byer II is my son. He is my son who died—suddenly and tragically. He is the son whom I carried, birthed, prayed for, raised, argued with, loved, and still love. His sudden and tragic death is a seismic event that has forever altered my existence. The acute sensations I felt when I received the news remain indelibly etched in my memory. There is no training, education, or instruction manual to prepare a person for this. There is no warning about what to avoid. I lament for my child who has died. Sometimes, the anatomy shifts in its progression across my heart. There is no remedy for this grief.

Grief is a capricious reprobate. One day it prompts laughter at fond memories of Arleigh, and the next, it incites an emotional breakdown. How could that be? I remember the baby boy whose dimples were so readily displayed because of how easily he laughed. He had a funny giggle that blossomed into a full-bellied laugh which eventually became the loud, ringing laughter we came to know, love, and tried to shush. When he smiled his joy came up through his eyes making them crinkle to accommodate the strength of his smile. It was a smile that made a person want to live. As a child, he had enough energy to run the entire village on and a love for public speaking. He never shied away from a performance and passionately advocated for anyone he perceived as being mistreated. He likely got that passion from me because for thirty-eight weeks, Arleigh was nestled in my womb surrounded by waters that were seasoned with a spirit of activism and stirred by the promise of good change.

Chapter 9

ARLEIGH WAS A VIBRANT and multifaceted individual: his infectious laughter, his artistic talents, and his public-speaking abilities were testament to that. He was fiercely independent which, though a mirror of my own personality, irritated me at times and was the cause of some of the disagreements between us. Many of those disagreements would sound something like this: In my best Darth Vader voice, I would remind him, "I am your mother." He in turn would reply, "Mommy I know that, but I know what I am doing. You just don't understand." I wonder: Is it just me, or does it bother anybody else that children often think that their parents don't understand (or know anything)?

During a visit home from Florida A&M University where he was a student, Arleigh sat me down for one of his signature heart-to-heart conversations, a setting where he often embraced the role of profound philosopher. Anticipating our usual dynamic exchange, I prepared myself mentally and emotionally. However, this discussion took an unexpectedly heartfelt turn.

In a moment of candid vulnerability, Arleigh expressed his deep admiration for the way I had raised him and his siblings. He earnestly confided, "Mommy, I boast to my friends about you. You came to this country and raised your four children by yourself without compromising yourself. I am so proud of you." This poignant confession continues to resonate with me, instilling a deep sense of respect for my son and a renewed pride in my own resilience and strength.

Following Arleigh's death, his friends expressed to me his admiration and love for me. They recounted how he often spoke highly of me, emphasizing his willingness to do anything for his mother. "Arleigh loved you so much," they said, a sentiment I echoed with heartfelt sincerity: "It is I who love Arleigh so much."

In another heart-to-heart conversation, Arleigh also shared his initial displeasure regarding our departure from Antigua. It emerged that, not having been privy to all the reasons behind this decision, he had formed his own assumptions. Fortunately, our subsequent conversations helped clarify the misgivings he carried, leading to a better mutual understanding. During our return to Antigua in 2016, I observed an unmistakable joy in him, although he maintained a composed demeanor, masking the depth of his happiness. It wasn't until this trip that I fully grasped the extent of his and his sister Arleigh-Ann's attachment to my homeland. Their enthusiasm was palpable, especially during the Carnival, Antigua's vibrant celebration of culture and emancipation. While Arleigh-Ann actively participated in the festivities, Arleigh seemed content to immerse himself in the atmosphere, absorbing the essence of our native culture. Earlier that year, Arleigh had promised to accompany her to the next Carnival. This unfulfilled promise remained a poignant memory for her after his death.

During our visit in 2016, when I was invited to preach at my home church in Antigua, I asked Arleigh to deliver a message to the youth. His work was impressive, filling me with pride. Despite his firm interest in pursuing a career in law, I harbored a secret hope that he might eventually choose the path of bold, prophetic preacher—a potential I saw in him, even if his own prayers were focused in a different direction.

Arleigh's connection to New York, his birthplace, remained strong, despite not having grown up there. This affinity manifested unexpectedly when, during his high school employment at Winn Dixie, I received an alarming call from New York. Initially frantic, I discovered that Arleigh had traveled there on a whimsical mission to "find me a husband." This revelation highlighted his protective nature and his close bond with my sister, who unwittingly became an accomplice in his plan.

Chapter 10

THIS STORY INDEED UNFOLDS like an intriguing tale. The initial encounter between Arleigh and Jerry (my husband) occurred in 2008 during a family trip to New York. We visited the city to revisit the hospital where my older children were born and to spend time with my sister who lived there. It was during this visit that Arleigh met Jerry for the first time, an encounter that was brief but evidently impactful. Unbeknownst to me, Jerry left a lasting impression on Arleigh, who years later embarked on a surprising mission to reunite Jerry and me.

To provide context, Jerry and I shared a romantic connection during our time in secondary school. Eventually, life led us in different directions, with Jerry moving to the US. Consequently, we lost contact and did not reunite until that brief encounter in 2008. I later discovered that, inspired by this meeting, my children had been secretly plotting to bring Jerry and me back together. Arleigh, in his characteristic protective manner, took it upon himself to actualize this plan.

My sister, unaware of Arleigh's intentions, found herself inadvertently involved when Arleigh persuaded her to assist in locating Jerry. After a meeting and discussion with Jerry in New York, Arleigh returned to Florida and continued his clandestine efforts with his siblings. He confided to me that from their first meeting, he and Arleigh-Ann felt that Jerry was an ideal match for me. It was only later that they learned of our history as high school sweethearts.

The culmination of this saga was both poignant and symbolic. Arleigh, having played a pivotal role in this journey, had the honor of walking me down the aisle on the day I married Jerry. The memory of his broad smile and palpable joy on that day remains an enduring source of happiness for me.

Chapter 11

IN MY ROLE AS a mother, I admit there were moments of imperfection. Often, when trying to call one of my children, whom I affectionately dubbed as the "Fantastic Four," I would mistakenly call them by each other's names. Their patience with this mix-up was not always steadfast, and they frequently expressed bewilderment at how I could confuse them. This puzzled me too, leading me to ponder the kind of mother who confuses her own children's names. The answer, it seems, is a mother like me.

A memorable incident occurred when I intended to call for Arleigha but mistakenly called for Arleigh. Upon his arrival, I acknowledged my error, apologized, and explained that I had meant to call his sister. Arleigh, with a hint of amusement, inquired, "Mommy, what's my name?" To which I confidently responded, "It's your name. You tell me." He pointed out many differences between the siblings, surprised by the mix-up, to which I replied, "You don't understand now, but when you become a mother, you will." His response, "You have jokes today, huh?" was met with my saucy, "All day long."

Despite the occasional missteps and mishaps, we have always maintained a tightly knit family dynamic, underpinned by mutual respect and an unwavering commitment to honesty and personal growth. Our family life is rich with joy and celebration, deeply ingrained in our cultural ethos of gathering around delicious food, set against the backdrop of a land known for its beautiful beaches, lively neighborhoods, and the ubiquitous and local friendly greetings, "Howdy!" and "Wah-a-gwarn!" Arleigh, though not one for dancing to calypso and soca music, enjoyed these moments in his own way, often humorously teased by Arleigh-Ann for his lack of dance skills, while Arleigha would dissolve into fits of laughter, cheering on his efforts. Despite his siblings' playful jibes, Arleigh remained content, dancing in his unique style, as long as he was close to the food.

Our adventures extended beyond family celebrations. When I acquired my first car in the US, it became a vessel for exploring local attractions, water parks, and more, often with my children's friends in tow, demonstrating their selfless nature. My Dodge Caravan served as our family vehicle and as a communal ride for many of their peers from the Blanche Ely High School marching band, ensuring no student was left stranded after practices or games as long as we could prevent it.

A poignant family anecdote involves Arleigh and the color red. Following his death, his school commemorated him by wearing red on his birthday. On this day, his brother Arleigho chose to wear Arleigh's red pants, which were oversized for him. Arleigho resourcefully researched ways to shrink the fabric to fit, and despite the imperfect fit, he wore them with a sense of pride and connection to his brother. Watching Arleigho don more of Arleigh's clothes and shoes, I recognized this as his way of processing his grief, preserving memories of his brother, and maintaining a bond with Arleigh's legacy.

Chapter 12

WHEN HE MOVED BACK to Broward from Tallahassee, Arleigh disengaged from traditional church practices. He confided in me, expressing his disillusionment, "I can't go back to that, Mommy. Church people really don't get it." Our conversations often revolved around his perceptions of the church's shortcomings and the disconnect he felt with conventional religious practices.

Despite his reluctance to participate in traditional Sunday services, Arleigh remained spiritually engaged, particularly in family studies. He saw himself as a "growing child of Yeshua," a testament to his evolving spiritual journey. In the summer leading up to his untimely death, he was actively leading his friends in a discussion on John 14. This involvement demonstrated his belief that a genuine connection with Jesus did not necessitate participation in what he viewed as "dusty, pretentious Sunday morning expressions." His approach to faith was deeply personal, prioritizing a sincere relationship over ritualistic practices he found disconnected from the true essence of the gospel.

Although it bothered me that Arleigh was not part of the congregation where I was serving or actively involved in any UMC congregation, I was at peace with the growth that I saw in him and excited about the conversations that we often shared around the Bible and theological concepts. He would not "go to church," but he would come and participate in specific areas when I requested his skill. I also understood his resistance to church culture and tried to keep my griping to a minimum—only about twice per month. His friends talked about his deep faith and that they have learned so much about God at work in the world by the way he treated them and the way they saw him treat the people he encountered. That's my child.

Chapter 13

ARLEIGH LIVED AND WORKED in Tallahassee after graduating from FAMU. He had started to study for the LSAT on his way to his dream vocation as an attorney who would fight on behalf of those caught up in the American injustice system. He talked about working with Equal Justice Initiative and was fascinated by the work that Bryan Stevenson was doing. While on the job he had in Tallahassee, he was called the n-word and was ready to physically respond to the racial slur. When he called me and told me about it, I offered my advice, which included leaving that work environment. I did not believe that a physical response would end well for my child, neither did I believe that reporting the behavior to the principals at his job would make a difference. Experience has shown that it rarely does.

Jerry was the one who proposed that Arleigh return to Broward to live with us. He planned to work, save for law school, and focus on his studies. To establish clear boundaries, I drafted an agreement to outline the terms of our cohabitation, now that he was returning as an adult. Upon reviewing it, Arleigh laughed and playfully inquired, "Are you sure you're not an attorney?" He agreed to adhere to most of the conditions, albeit humorously declining to formally sign the document. His stubbornness was evident even in this.

Living together was generally enjoyable, except for Arleigh's extraordinary appetite. I recall a day when he returned from teaching eighth grade English at Margate Middle School and walked into the kitchen where I was cooking. "It smells wonderful in here!" he exclaimed with his characteristic flair for the dramatic. "What's that you're cookin' good-lookin'?" he asked boisterously. "Spicy mushrooms," I responded, amused. His playful protest, "Nonsense. How could you do this to me? It smells like chicken. You have betrayed me, Mommy!" was followed by his infectious laughter. Despite his theatrics, he ate more of those mushrooms than I did, before heading to his room to study.

For over a year after his death, I found myself unable to make the bed he used. Earlier on the day he died, he had laundered his clothes but hadn't yet stripped his bed. Lying there, I would try to capture his scent and imagine his laughter while watching TV in his room—one of the rules he disregarded. Discovering my mason jars in his room indicated his habit of sneaking food and drinks, another breach of our household norms.

Similarly, sorting through his belongings was a hurdle I couldn't overcome. I could touch his items, but moving them felt impossible. While retrieving a laptop from his bag for Margate Middle School, the overwhelming sense of loss engulfed me again. The sight of his bag and shoes evoked memories of his morning routine and the sound of his footsteps in the hallway as he left for work. I fondly recall insisting on a hug one morning, to which he responded with a sheepish grin and an embrace. His playful spontaneity, like the time he mischievously slapped my bottom and darted away, declaring, "It had to be done!" is a cherished memory that brings his laughter back to me, in his absence.

Arleigh's death leaves an irreplaceable void in my life. The passage of time since that fateful day, August 24, 2019, has not diminished the deep pain that I feel. Regardless of what the future holds, even in the face of potential memory loss, the love shared between us, and the pain of his absence, will forever be etched in my heart. I will never forget my son and the memories we created together.

Chapter 14

*"Who smashed my body into so many pieces?
I am looking for the pieces, and I cannot find them."*
(Journal excerpt)

Grief and My Body

IN HIS BOOK *THE Body Keeps the Score* author Bessel van der Kolk says that we can't get better until we "know what we know and feel what we feel."[1] When my son died, my body went into shock according to the doctor. My body began to act in ways that were unfamiliar to me. My womb hurt. Sometimes, it still throbs spontaneously as if getting ready to give birth, and I get the urge to bear down. I think of this as giving birth to my grief and allowing myself to become familiar with it. There is a cold bleakness that still rests on my belly and tugs at my breasts as if to taunt me. Immediately following Arleigh's death, my breasts would get full and when they were not treated as nursing breasts usually are, they spilled their contents in angry bursts. The first time this happened, I freaked out! I felt the tightness and my memory returned to 1994 when my first child was born, and I experienced this sensation for the first time. My therapist later told me that this is a normal reaction. Normal. What does

---

1. Van der Kolk, *Body Keeps the Score*, 26.

that mean anymore? I have no words, for when the body feels so much pain, words cannot keep pace.

It makes sense that grief will show up in the body to speak. After all, God used the body for incarnation. Since salvation is embodied, there is no reason why grief, being part of the human story, would be so different. Grief cannot be over spiritualized. Grief is hell, and grieving is salvific. It is both individual and communal. On the anniversary of my son's death, my body refused to let my mind skip out. I remember everything. I remember when the news of my son's death landed in my ears, how my heart rose up to kick its arse.

After Arleigh's death, I lost my appetite entirely. Food turned into an unpalatable burden, leaving a bitter taste in my mouth and my stomach perpetually empty. It felt like my body was slowly wasting away, starved of sustenance. Then, almost unexpectedly, months later, my appetite returned with a vengeance, and I found myself eating incessantly. It was as if a switch had been flipped, and I couldn't stop. My weight fluctuated, playing a relentless game of gain and loss. Nausea and dry heaves tormented me, especially when I had to venture outside.

In the days and months immediately following Arleigh's death, my voice, too, seemed to vanish. I had to coax it back, like calling out to a lost friend. I had so many words in my head. All of which seemed to bottle-neck in my throat. When I opened my mouth, nothing came out except for the keening that my ears were getting tired of hearing.

The thought of leaving the safety of home filled me with dread. I carried an unshakable fear that I might not return, and I couldn't bear the thought of causing my family more pain. Mornings when the children had to go to school or Jerry had to leave for work were the worst. My stomach would twist and turn, and my anxiety would peak. I did not want any of us to leave. Arleigh-Ann, my eldest, lived in Tampa at the time, and she would make the long drive back and forth just so we could be together. But each time she got on the road to come home, my heart would race erratically. You see, I knew firsthand that there are callous individuals with driver's licenses.

Grief, it's worth noting, is not the refined and composed performance one might see on a stage. It is a messy, turbulent force that can wreak havoc on your life. Sleep abandoned me, and insomnia became a relentless companion. Months later, I reluctantly filled a prescription for a sleeping aid. It knocked me out entirely, even though I had only taken a small fraction of the pill. After less than a week, I stopped taking it because the aftereffects left me feeling too lethargic to function. Since then, sleep has mostly eluded me, and when it does come, it often brings nightmares with it. What is "normal" in the face of such upheaval?

In the midst of these trials, my eyesight also significantly worsened, a witness to the fact that the body's response to trauma is not always visibly apparent, yet its impact is acute and active. Initially, I was unaware that the further decline in my vision was connected to the trauma my body and mind were enduring. It was only during a routine check-up, a year later, with the ophthalmologist that I began to understand the correlation.

During the examination, the ophthalmologist inquired about any recent traumatic experiences. Overwhelmed, my eyes brimmed with tears, and I revealed the heartrending result of my son's accident. The ophthalmologist responded with empathy, "Ah, that explains it. The trauma from your son's death has significantly impacted your eye health. I'm so sorry about your son." This moment was a stark realization of how deeply grief can ravage one's physical well-being, a painful yet enlightening truth about the far-reaching effects of heavy sorrow.

The arm that once cradled Arleigh, my chubby baby, still throbs with the memory. His weight strained my right arm and shoulder back then. The memory and pain in the arm now serve as a painful reminder that I will never carry or hug him again. My entire body is a memory.

Sometimes, it's as if gravity itself is toying with me, shifting up and down, up, and down. My body oscillates between heaviness and lightness, constantly forcing me to recalibrate.

PART 1: PERSONAL STORIES

I share these experiences to acknowledge them as part of my story. This is not a prescription for how the body should behave in the face of trauma. Grief takes on countless forms, unique to each person. I must grapple with the pain of my child Arleigh's death in my own way. The body keeps score, and it can be a ruthless and remarkable scorekeeper. It remembers, it challenges, and it signals us in various ways and languages. Post-traumatic stress syndrome (PTSS) is one of its languages.

Chapter 15

PTSS IS OFTEN ASSOCIATED with combat. However, trauma is not limited to war zones. Both my doctor and therapist informed me that I had PTSS. According to the American Psychological Association, trauma is an emotional response to a harrowing event, like (but not limited to) an accident, rape, or natural disaster. Initially, shock and denial are common reactions, followed by unpredictable emotions, flashbacks, strained relationships, and even physical symptoms like headaches or nausea. This, of course, doesn't cover the full spectrum of trauma and its effects.

When flowers and sympathy cards started pouring in following my child's death, my anger flared. I did not want anyone talking to me about the death of my child. They used phrases like "Sorry for your loss." Loss? What does that even mean? As the flowers began to wither, I felt a deep-seated sense of defeat. They stood there, decaying, taunting me, as a reminder that Arleigh was gone.

One Sunday, as I resumed pastoral duties after Arleigh's death, we neared the end of the worship service, just after sharing communion. A motorcycle roared by outside. In the past, I would have heard that sound and silently whispered a prayer for the rider's safety (I never liked motorcycles). But that day, it was the specific sound of the motorcycle that unraveled me completely, and I scolded myself for being vulnerable in a place where my heart should have felt safe. This thought would eventually catapult me to action and set me on a different course with the congregation that I served at the time.

I harbored a deep-seated hope that Arleigh would return, walking through the door with his characteristic grin, exclaiming, "It had to be done!" This wishful thinking was a desire I clung to fervently. I would often find myself imagining forgiving him for what I wished was just a cruel prank. Yet, the sound of his laughter, which I longed for, never materialized again; it resonated only within the confines of my heart. The harsh reality was that Arleigh was no longer with us.

One night, I dreamed he was there in the house annoying his siblings like he believed it was his life's work to do. When one of them called for me to come rescue them, I went running in like the mommy cavalry that I am. He turned to me, taking the boxer's stance, and asked with his grin, "What you think you doing, Mommy?" "Whooping your behind," I replied, without relaxing my stance. "You really believe that?" came back his saucy response. Then he laughed. And just like that, the dream was over, he was gone, and I was awakened feeling angry and hurt. My son was gone.

Chapter 16

ARLEIGH DIED ON A Saturday. The stark reality hit me when I inquired, "Where is Arleigh? I want to see him," only to be told, "Your son is with the medical examiner." There was no hospital intervention for Arleigh because, as I was informed, "Arleigh died at the scene of the accident." The inability to see my son in those moments was agonizing. Driven by a desperate need to see him, I urged Jerry as soon as he woke up on Sunday to take me to the medical examiner's office. Unfamiliar with the processes surrounding such situations and unwilling to wait, we found out upon our arrival that the office was closed for the weekend. The delay in seeing my son felt interminable, each moment stretching out endlessly.

The long-awaited call came on Monday, and my impatience was such that the car seemed unbearably slow. I had visited the funeral home previously with others and was acquainted with its environment. Yet, on that day, the room felt constricting as an alien space where my body seemed unable to fit. Before I could see Arleigh, there were selections to be made and paperwork to complete. My signature, rendered unrecognizable by my trembling hand, reflected my inner turmoil.

Despite the funeral director's gentleness, I found myself internally railing against the absurdity of the situation, wanting to plead, "Don't you understand that this is my son?" My son was there, no longer part of this world.

I walked into the room where Arleigh's body lay on a raised platform, and the sight of him unraveled me once more. "What is happening to me?" I remember asking aloud. Arleigh was wrapped from his shoulders to his feet, his hands positioned by his sides, immobile. My cries for him to "Get up, Arleigh" were met with an agonizing silence. No amount of touching or coaxing stirred him. His stillness was a painful reminder of the stubbornness he once had in life.

Chapter 17

IN THE WAKE OF a child's death, it becomes a practical necessity, albeit a heart-wrenching one, to remove them as a beneficiary from life insurance policies and similar arrangements. The gravity of this task was overwhelming. It took several attempts before I could muster the strength to articulate this change. It was one of the most painful tasks that I ever had to do, and for many days after the phone calls, I could not leave my bed. The weeks and months following the devastating confirmation of Arleigh's death involved additional burdens: the strenuous process of notifying insurance companies, the Social Security Administration, and other entities. Particularly distressing was the visit to the school board. Triggers lurked everywhere, and for a long time, for me, a knock on the door meant that the police were arriving with the terrible news. Do they ever bring good news, anyway?

People often advise me to hold onto the memories I have of Arleigh. And I do. However, memories feel like a meager consolation, or a pale shadow in comparison to the vibrant life he led. The transition from having a living, breathing child to referring to them as memories is a jarring one. This reality has led me to fervently wish for the longevity of my other children, a desire for them to outlive even my wildest dreams. Arleigh was alive, vibrantly so, until the moment he wasn't.

Chapter 18

*I am weary with my moaning;
every night I flood my bed with tears.*

—Psalm 6:6

*Suppressing the Lament: Personal Experience,
Caribbean Culture, and the Church*

PART OF THE IMPORTANCE of writing this book arises from my own deeply personal encounters with trauma and my responses to these experiences. These narratives are placed in dialogue with the historical reactions of the worshiping community concerning trauma and lament within the context of divine worship. Regrettably, the responses of my worshiping community often felt shallow, providing more harm than healing. While I acknowledge the cultural factors that shaped these responses, I am determined to challenge the notion that faith in God and a whispered prayer alone are sufficient to navigate the complexities of trauma. The suppression of our pain, I firmly believe, harms both ourselves and those around us.

In the colonized and post-colonized Antigua, where my grandmother lived and breathed, there was scant room for the open expression of grief. This legacy traces back to the era when slavers and colonizers held sway, viewing human lives on the islands through the lens of profit margins. Stories were passed down of our ancestors enduring severe mistreatment and dehumanization at the hands of the slavers who owned their flesh. Women gave birth in unforgiving fields, denied the chance to nurture their own bodies, instead coerced to return to toil immediately. Death, in this unforgiving reality, did little to disrupt the relentless rhythm of existence. Granny recounted stories from her mother of enslaved individuals, having suffered brutal whippings, being forced to don disguises and sing. This forced semblance of life mirrors the haunting imagery of the Babylonian captors demanding a song from their captives (Ps 137).

Fast forward through the generations, and the suppression of lament becomes the rule, not the exception, in how Caribbean people contend with trauma. In those bygone days, the Christian community exhibited limited emotional awareness, emotional intelligence, or emotional acumen. Tragically, it appears that only a little has evolved in this regard. Instead of fostering healthy channels for processing pain, the Christian community largely chooses to stifle suffering with vacuous platitudes that insinuate that grieving is equal to a lack of faith. When my mother died, "Don't cry," they said. "Your mother is now in a better place." "Just trust in God." The list of well-intentioned yet misguided counsel I received stretched longer than I could have ever imagined, forming a noose by which my grieving heart felt strangled.

Then came the sudden death of my grandmother in 2010, shared in a heartbreaking Sunday morning phone call as I was preparing to attend the 10:00 a.m. worship service at my congregation in the United States. "Andrea, Granny passed away this morning." My Granny and I shared a bond that transcended the ordinary. We were inseparable, like the most perfect pairs—chap-up and saltfish, blouse and skirt, and shoes and socks. You get the picture. The news of her death struck me like a hurricane. At the time, I was residing in the United States, while she resided in Antigua. We had spoken just the day before, and she concluded our conversation as she always did: "I love you, Andrea. Trust in the Lord with all your heart and lean not on your own understanding. Andrea, in all your ways acknowledge God and God will direct your path." Each time I read or hear Prov 3:5–6, her voice echoes in my mind. It was her mantra and guiding principle of life, and I could almost hear her emphasizing, "Trust in the Lord with ALL your heart."

Chapter 19

GRANNY'S DEATH RESURRECTED THE anguish I felt when my mother died. It was as though my mother's death had occurred all over again. While I grappled with this renewed crisis, the well-meaning but familiar advice from the church community in the US echoed the sentiments I had heard after my mother's death in Antigua: "Don't cry," "You must be strong," and so on. Months after her death, as I watched a recording of Granny's funeral service, I remember sinking deeper and deeper into the blankets enveloping me. In hindsight, it wasn't until I could no longer see the television screen that I realized how much I had physically distanced myself from the apparent finality of the funeral.

Under the weight of cultural expectations, and despite the tears that flowed freely for an extended period, I unknowingly stifled the pain. However, when the most recent death struck—the death of my own child—I could no longer contain it. I made a conscious choice to grant myself the gift of lament, to acknowledge the tearing of my heart, and to beseech God to respond in some way.

Chapter 20

*"O my son (Arleigh), my son, my son Arleigh!
Would I had died instead of you, O Arleigh,
my son, my son!"* (based on 2 Samuel 18:33)

Releasing the Lament: Personal Experience

EVEN NOW, YEARS HAVE passed, yet speaking, sharing, or writing about this remains an agonizing undertaking that pierces my heart. There was nothing obvious in the events of that day, leading up to that fateful moment, to suggest the impending catastrophe. On that Saturday morning, my son Arleigh was bustling about, cleaning his room, doing laundry, scheduling an oil change for my car, and reminding my husband Jerry to prepare the meal he had requested. And let me tell you, when Arleigh ate, it was no small feat. With the appetite of several people, he could outeat anyone at the table.

His eulogy, though heartfelt, fell short of capturing his essence. Arleigh exuded such vibrancy that it simultaneously frightened and invigorated me. I distinctly recall the story behind the small scar on his stomach. His fearlessness was legendary within our family, and I often found myself nervously clenching my buttocks because he wasn't afraid to confront certain situations head-on, situations I would rather address with a pen. Don't misunderstand me; he was far from reckless. In truth, he was likely less reckless than I am. While I wielded the pen in a seemingly passive arc, my pen could be sharp, cutting multiple ways.

Like me, Arleigh constantly championed the underdog. Injustice infuriated him, and any act of one human transgressing against another deeply disturbed him. When the family participated in protests against structural racism following the murder of George Floyd, his absence left a palpable void, for his presence and energy were sorely missed.

Arleigh embraced life fully. His existence, from babyhood to adulthood, reverberated with energy and resonated at a loud octave. As he matured, his voice acquired a deep, sultry timbre. Yet his laughter, characterized by its exuberance, remained boisterous, infectious, and capable of brightening even the bleakest moments. Arleigh never shied away from embracing his authentic self; he refused to hold back. Since his death, I've found myself leaning into one of his critiques of me: "Mommy, you care too much about what other people think. Every time you 'tone down' to appease someone else, you rob yourself. You'll always be 'too much' for somebody. Forget them. They're just miserable. Miserable, I tell you!" Then he'd burst into laughter, that resounding, uproarious laughter that could wake up the entire neighborhood.

Chapter 21

It was Saturday, August 24, 2019, just one week shy of Arleigh's twenty-fourth birthday on August 30. I glanced out of a window from my makeshift workspace and noticed figures dressed like police officers, along with one other person out of uniform, making their way to my front door. Oddly, my typically cautious mind did not prepare me for any suspicion. It felt as though my thoughts had retreated, leaving me in a state of eerie calm. I returned to the task at hand, bottling a fragrance I had spent the past month crafting for Arleigh's upcoming birthday. I was in the process of creating a line of skincare products, each individual product scented with this special fragrance. I loved it! After countless adjustments, I had finally achieved a scent that encapsulated his essence—deep, vibrant, rooted, and alive.

There was a knock at the door, urging me to shift my focus. I opened it, offering a welcoming smile to my guests. One of the uniformed officers remained outside. I was asked to sit down, specifically next to the individual out of uniform who introduced herself as the "victim advocate." The other officer identified himself by name and proceeded to deliver the heart-wrenching news of Arleigh's death. I heard phrases like, "You know that your mother has died right?" and "Andrea, Granny passed away this morning." Then, the words that shattered my world: "Arleigh died at the scene of the accident."

I watched my pain, which had been dormant, suddenly surge past the reserve of stoicism to color the entire room the color of a fresh horrible wound! The room, which had just been filled with the fragrance of my labor, the scent of fresh laundry, Jerry's cooking, and the warmth of a happy home, now reeked of staleness, futility, and the ebbing of my life. "Arleigh died at the scene of the accident." I had seen Arleigh so full of life not too long ago. Can someone rewind this nightmare and edit it, please? Is that my own voice crying? Yes, it is. "Arleigh died at the scene of the accident." "Is anyone else hurt?" I managed to inquire at some point. "No." "Arleigh died at the scene of the accident." It wasn't like him to leave without saying, "Bye Mommy. I love you." That's our family's practice. Yet, what I was being told was that he had left without a farewell. I did not get to say goodbye. There was no banter about his outfit. "Arleigh died at the scene of the accident." It sounded absurd because Arleigh would never do this. His birthday was just a week away. However, the police and the victim advocate insisted that, absurd as it sounded, it was true.

Chapter 22

IN THE AFTERMATH OF this life-altering moment, the local church's response to my grief mirrored the reactions I had encountered after the deaths of my mother and grandmother. This time, though, I was the pastor. People were not prepared for a pastor's grief, and I certainly was not prepared for the death of my son. What the hell? Who could ever be prepared for such a tragedy? I found myself by the waters of my personal Babylon, weeping, lamenting, and questioning God—all things discouraged by my Afro-Caribbean culture. I refused to accept shallow, religious responses from well-meaning individuals. Instead, I bared my soul to God, showing her the depths of my pain.

The church's expectation was that I would quickly "recover," fueled by the belief that as a pastor, my grief should remain less conspicuous. Some accused me of weakness, and others whispered that I had "lost" my faith. Some who visited me were disappointed by my silence. They had anticipated words of encouragement and wisdom, simply because I was a pastor. All I had to offer was my pain. Seemingly, they all forgot that I was, first, human.

We've been conditioned to perceive vulnerability as a sign of weakness, and I deeply regret that this is our reality. It deprives us of the growth that emerges from confronting life's most formidable challenges. Our societal conditioning has also led us to believe that every problem has a solution, and if we search diligently enough, these neatly categorized answers will reveal themselves.

Yet, when an experience arises that defies our usual interpretive categories, reflection becomes an arduous task. When my son died, I could not bring myself to reflect. I did not even want to. Arleigh's death was no ordinary event in my family's life. I could not find comfort in the customary religious platitudes that people often employ during such times—and I still can't. I had no reflections to share. My heart was overflowing with lamentation. There was no orderly, filtered structure to the thoughts and words that poured forth. They were raw, and each word seared my throat, demanding to be released.

In the days following Arleigh's death, my innermost thoughts began to take on an artistic form. (Of course, they did! They were my thoughts, and that's how they emerged!) My thoughts flowed out of me as if driven by a frantic force, and as they spilled forth, they stunned some who heard them. I could not contain them even if I had wanted to; they refused to be silenced. "No!" my thoughts cried out. "You won't do yourself any good by keeping us locked away. Release us."

So, I did.

My Lament for My Son

I saw the pain
I heard the hurt
I felt the disdain that ricocheted
Around the room filled with gloom
And I could not help but assume
That the scene to which my eyes were glued
Was the story of my own becoming.
There is no sound from over there
I am listening but all I hear
Is the sound of tears echoing in the silence.
What is your answer to the threat
That is making me wet
With tears and sweat sunup to sunset?
Nothing.
Nothing? Do you not have anything to
Sing, to say, to offer my way? When I incline my ear
For the sound of your voice, there is nothing.
Hello?
Are you there?
Can you hear?
I am calling, but you are stalling

TEARS AT THE ALTAR, LAMENT IN MY BREASTS

Do you not see your people bawling
In despair? Do you not hear? Do you not care?
I am picking a fight, but your lips are locked
Tight
As if
I am nothing
As if
I am a bug just buzzing. I am pumping
Pumping for a fight but your lips are locked
Tight.
I am hopping, puffing, stunting, jumping, bucking
I am not bluffing.
Say something! God!
Say something. Answer. Argue. Talk back.
Cut me some slack
So I can go back
And tell my family, that yes you are here.
I keep hearing that you are there
But where? Where is your voice?
The one I used to rejoice
By choice
About your faithfulness? Where are you God?
Cat got your tongue—Hushed up your song?
Answer! Is it morning yet, Lord?
They said that in the morning we can rejoice.
Is it morning yet?
Then when will it get here
And chase away the tears

That are always so near?

They tell me that you collect tears in a bottle.

How big is your bottle? Is it strong enough

To bear the weight of my pain?

Weeping is enduring. Is it morning yet?

Weeping is enduring . . . weeping

Help Lord. Gather the scattered. I know no other

Who will bother

To stoop to the lowly. The lowly is leaning into your redeeming.

You are my God and I love you . . . I think. Help me!!!

Chapter 23

THE ECONOMY OF GRIEF operates on an exchange that necessitates a deliberate confrontation. While many were taken aback that I, a pastor, would both grieve and publicly express this lament, I later realized that by permitting myself, I was, in fact, paving the way for others to confront their own traumas and embark on their healing journeys.

In my lament, I plunge into a multitude of emotions that have traversed my life. I must admit that some of these emotions took me by surprise, forcing me to confront the depths of my own humanity. However, they have also liberated me in ways I had not experienced before. My complex Afro-Caribbean heritage continues to shape my approach to my pain. At times, I embrace it wholeheartedly; at other times, I resist its influence. It provides a rich tapestry of cultural references that inform my language and guide my actions as I embody my theology in the world. This lament itself is an act of defiance against the very heritage that molded my more formative years and the pressure to conceal my painful realities. Since the environment of my upbringing failed to accommodate such expressions, I chose to carve out my own space. The pain I endure following my child's death cannot be soothed with simple phrases like "God knows best." I find no need to make excuses for God, for I firmly believe that God's vastness, depth, and decency allow her to encompass all of this while remaining a benevolent God, despite life's tumultuous circumstances.

Chapter 24

My son died during the same week I commenced my doctoral work at Candler School of Theology. Between the program's inception and conclusion, my pastoral context underwent two significant changes. These shifts have added various dimensions to my grief. I grieved not only because the first move was necessary to facilitate my healing but also because the second relocation was more drastic, taking me out of the county and physically distancing me from individuals I had known and connected with over the years. My youngest child, Arleigho, who had formed vital friendships at school and relied on them as a source of support following his brother's death, struggled immensely with adapting to this unfamiliar and not altogether kind environment.

For us, the sense of strangeness is further heightened by the new elements in our lives: orange and yellow striped lizards, frogs greeting us at the front door, flags promoting Trumpism, armadillos roaming nearby, individuals donning "Go Brandon" T-shirts during an event held in the church sanctuary, bunnies playfully hopping across our front lawn, and the ultimate surprise—bobcats in our backyard! What in the name of third creation is this? Bobcats in our backyard!

However, beyond these quirky occurrences, the required adjustment process begins with an acknowledgment of the unfamiliarity that surrounds us.

Chapter 25

Personal Struggles

THERE ARE MOMENTS WHEN I grapple with guilt over Arleigh's death. An intimidating sense bullies me, telling me that, as his mother, I should have shielded him from death. I am aware of the irrationality in such thoughts. Some days, I succeed in this internal struggle; on others days, the struggle overwhelms me. The mind can be a tricky adversary. Similarly, I combat feelings of guilt surrounding my mother's death. Why didn't I have the resources to provide her with the medical care she needed? Why didn't I push harder to secure the funds? I understand the irrationality of these sentiments. Some days, I emerge victorious in this battle; other days, the battle conquers me. The mind can play tricks.

Depression is a very real and potent force, and it is not a matter of choice. One cannot simply pray it away. Depression does not always manifest in conventional ways either. Just as no two people grieve identically, depression wears different masks. Sometimes, a person battling depression can function at their workplace but struggle in other aspects of life. They may engage in some activities but find others overwhelmingly challenging. Since Arleigh's death, I can still deliver a sermon or other speech in front of a congregation or audience of any size, but I now feel anxious being in crowds or up close with people. However, I experience no anxiety when I'm shopping at Ross or Old Time Pottery, browsing the plant nursery, exploring the craft store, or shaking up on the dance floor. These encounters, though sharing common elements, evoke distinct emotions.

We often affirm the infinite grace of God, which reaches us in our unique situations. Examining scriptural studies and participating in discussions about lament as a form of worship has highlighted the necessity for well-defined guidelines for creating room for people's pain. These guidelines would assist the faith community in responding genuinely and faithfully to life's traumatic events.

The church should embrace its authenticity by allowing space for the articulation of human trauma within communal worship, rather than attempting to shield God from life's harsh realities. It is essential to move beyond the notion of leaving one's troubles at the sanctuary's door. Part of this transformative process could include engaging with psalms of lament as well as imprecatory psalms such as Ps 137. Such engagement could alleviate the discomfort associated with expressing pain and anger toward God, facilitating a journey from feelings of displacement to a sense of re-placement.

In the wake of my son Arleigh's death, I was consumed by anger, an emotion that persists. This anger was directed toward God for not averting the tragedy, the irresponsible driver responsible for Arleigh's death, and the church's failure to provide space for my grief. My once robust prayer life dwindled as I struggled to converse with a God who seemed indifferent and harsh. Thus, suppression was not a viable option for me.

Acknowledging the existence and influence of anger, loss, and trauma is crucial not only for working through grief but also for enriching the celebratory dimension of worship. By recognizing these intense emotions, we facilitate a deeper, more intimate engagement with the divine covenant that God has established with humanity.

Salvation, as envisioned by God, includes the aspiration for humanity to rise above suffering, but not through its glorification or evasion. The late theologian Walter Wink asserted our connection with all life, highlighting the inevitability of feeling the world's pervasive pain.[1] He contended that the continuous wave of global suffering affects us profoundly, emphasizing that avoidance is futile. We are compelled to confront and carry this collective burden of suffering, necessitating a language to express our deep-seated distress and present it before God. The heart at the universe's core alone has the capacity to endure such immense pain. Hastening from lament to praise diminishes the depth of our engagement with God and overlooks the profundity of an intimate covenant. Our religious traditions, platitudes, and a superficial reading of Scripture fall short of providing true solace if we sidestep the vital, humanizing, and therapeutic journey of lament.

Grief intrusively affects every facet of our existence. Reflecting on Ps 139:7–8, the psalmist's query captures the essence of grief's pervasive nature, which can find and displace us simultaneously. Grief operates independently of scholarly interpretations or societal norms, adhering to its own trajectory, much like Arleigh's candid assertion that "[Grief] won't give a rat's furry butt."

Grief eschews platitudes and rehearsed sentiments, not seeking justification but rather embracing the agony, exposing the scars, and acknowledging the void. It manifests a distinct awareness, heightening our sense of existence and the spaces we inhabit, and it underscores the clash between authenticity and conventional expectations. Traditional or systematic knowledge is inadequate for navigating grief's complexities; it is a phenomenon unto itself.

While grief weighs heavily upon us, lament as a form of worship acts as a liberator from this burden. Lament, in its unadulterated essence, does not concern itself with sanitizing its expression for divine presentation. It remains indifferent to the preferences of a church that avoids confronting harsh realities, instead calling for a forthright engagement with grief, its intricate aspects, and the pursuit of transformation. Lament recognizes the multidimensional nature of grief and asserts its autonomous path.

---

1. See Wink, *Engaging the Powers*.

Chapter 26

I HAVE RELINQUISHED MY expectations of how others should react to suffering. Following my son's death, my aspiration was for people to see beyond my pastoral role and recognize my grief as a mother. I yearned for their understanding that my life had been irrevocably altered, rendering me shattered and incapable of dealing with my son's death dispassionately. I anticipated empathy and kindness without the expectation of reciprocation, hoping my sorrow would not lead to isolation but would be met with genuine affection.

The misconception of my persona as almost superhuman was perhaps held by some, leading to their astonishment when confronted with my humanity. Their reaction of "Wow! The woman pastor is human after all!" prompts me to consider whether my endeavors to rectify every problem and promote well-being might have inadvertently shaped this perception.

A notable incident occurred when I ran into a church member at the grocery store, whose surprise at seeing me in such a mundane setting prompted introspection about public perceptions of my role. Despite my pastoral responsibilities, I partake in everyday activities akin to those of others. I've come to understand that there's a delicate balance between releasing people from unrealistic expectations and insisting on improved conduct. My approach has matured; while I no longer presume that people understand how to interact with someone immersed in grief, I expect that with guidance on appropriate and supportive behavior, they will adapt accordingly.

Since Arleigh's death, protecting my emotional and mental well-being has become paramount. Occasionally, distancing myself from individuals with whom I shared a bond is painful yet imperative. This stance is a departure from my mother's practice of tolerating disrespect while outwardly appearing content, a behavior Arleigh critiqued. In tribute to his memory, I work through the ongoing challenges posed by his death, committed to making choices that honor my emotional integrity and dignity.

Chapter 27

I HAD A CONVERSATION with a widow who had buried her husband's body, just a week prior to our discussion. She conveyed her deep distress, recounting an encounter with another member of her congregation. This individual had suggested that the widow needed to release her emotional attachment to her departed husband. The reasoning behind this counsel was the belief that failure to do so would hinder her husband's peaceful rest. The widow was overwhelmed by guilt, grappling with the idea that her grief might be preventing her late husband, with whom she had shared a deep and enduring love for over two decades, from finding tranquility in the afterlife.

In her state of distress, she articulated her inner turmoil, seeking guidance: "How can I let go of him as though he never existed?" she wailed. "How can I simply cease to love him and stop missing him? I do not want to hinder his rest, but I don't know what to do."

To state that I was angry at the petty, deeply insensitive, and borderline vicious advice is to put my feelings very mildly. It is entirely natural for this widow to miss her late spouse. Not only that, the feelings of missing him would persist. This poor woman does not possess the agency to dictate her husband's eternal rest. It was tough helping the widow to correct the notion that her grief could obstruct his repose and that the suggestion of her fellow church member, was fundamentally illogical. Grief has a way of eclipsing logic, particularly when one is ensnared in its throes.

Chapter 28

So, what then is our response to the pain of our loved one's death?

We should respond in the way that is most helpful to us, not the way anyone thinks we should. Our salvation is not in silent suffering. For me, I am learning the language that I need to speak, and I am speaking it. It is a language as old as the Scriptures and as new as my latest breath. It is the language of lament. To lose the language of lament is to force us humans to ignore our humanity; it is to diminish authenticity and invite self-and-communal debasement. It is basically lobotomizing our faith and snatching the freedom that I believe God gives us to express our woundedness. We are no less blessed for naming the mess. Neither are we more blessed for ignoring the stress. The blessing may be in naming these. It is an act of mercy—to self and to the world.

I am observing my other children negotiate this constantly new, consistently rough, and excruciatingly long season of their lives. They miss their brother. They hurt. I hurt because they hurt. They hurt because I hurt. It is a cyclical hell. Children also need deep support in times of trauma. I do not want my children to believe the fallacy that God must not be questioned. I have long since apologized to them for any way that I may have contributed to this unrealistic orientation. However, it seemed they were ahead of me. They are emotionally competent and intelligent beings who do not share my residual emotional incompetence. In addition, my husband is learning new ways to love me through the new places of pain, even as he processes the hurt that he too feels at Arleigh's death. I am learning new ways to love him as well. Our family has been impacted by this trauma forever. And until Jesus comes, Arleigh's death will shape our realities.

Part 2
Bible Talk

Chapter 29

I WANT TO CREATE life-giving, ethical, moral spaces at the intersection of the biblical narrative and the here and now. I have chosen several passages of Scripture that speak to the raw and unfiltered experiences of human suffering, loss, and the struggle to find meaning in the midst of it all. I find that these passages are often read quickly or glossed over in traditional settings, even though they hold deep reservoirs of grief, questioning, and, ultimately, the possibility of renewal—sometimes.

Each passage has been chosen for its ability to connect us with the realities of those moments when life doesn't make sense, when the weight of sorrow feels unbearable, and when we are left standing in the gap between despair and hope. Through these scriptures, we will investigate how lament is not limited to a personal cry but can be a powerful act of worship, or at least a sacred space where we can confront the complexities of life and faith.

They bring us face to face with the raw agony of a person who loses everything including children; voices in the Psalms crying out from the depth of despair, anger, and fear; the story of women moving back and forth through geographical and emotional spaces; the weeping of Jesus at his friend's tomb and in the garden of Gethsemane; the Levite's treatment of his concubine; the rape of Bathsheba; the rape of Tamar; and Mother Mary's presence at the cross of Jesus.

Taken together, the chosen passages offer a textured and honest portrayal of what it can mean to live through unspeakable suffering, to lament, and to find language to express both.

Chapter 30

Trauma, the Church, Lament, and the Bible:
Building a Wailing Wall

ANY EXAMINATION OF TRAUMA, which is a topic of major significance, should invariably lead us to the Bible. The Bible, serving as a critical touchstone, is frequently at the epicenter of discussions, whether they revolve around controversial or conventional matters, although these categories are inherently subjective. This prominence can be attributed to the Bible's status as one of the most significant and potent books ever compiled and published. Furthermore, its pages contain numerous accounts of trauma, as many of its scriptures were crafted in the aftermath of traumatic experiences such as exile and enslavement. Within the framework of a firmly held belief that God embodies both goodness and grace, the authors of the Old and New Testaments grappled with acute questions pertaining to trauma, evil, suffering, grief, and related themes.

Consequently, various genres in the Bible, including historical narratives, legal codes, prophetic writings, wisdom literature, apocalyptic texts, the Gospels, and Epistles, have made efforts to engage with these turbulent waters. Paradoxically, certain pietistic practices within worshiping communities have elevated grief, trauma, and suffering to the status of divine life lessons, inadvertently rendering the act of acknowledging these realities, feeling and naming them in lament, as acts of disrespect toward God.

However, it's imperative not to overlook the examples set by biblical writers who, at times, refrained from veiling their own history of oppression, exile, participation in the displacement of other nations, the specter of Roman occupation, and the perilous endeavors and ultimate lynching of Jesus. These instances emphasize the nuanced approach taken by the Bible itself toward the matter of trauma and suffering.

The church has cultivated a repertoire of clichés, such as "I am too blessed to be stressed," "Life is hard, but God is good," and "Faith over fear," seemingly in an attempt to stifle the expression of lament. Regrettably, my experiences, particularly within Caribbean churches, have revealed the removal of lament from the church's vocabulary. These clichés insinuate that trauma and grief are antagonistic and abusive forces. I contend that grief can indeed manifest as adversarial and abusive. Avoiding or attempting to wash over life-altering events in worship, rather than confronting them, often lulls individuals into a false sense of well-being. Phrases like "Faith over fear" prove insufficient when life takes an unforeseen turn.

Chapter 31

JOHN 11 PROVIDES AN emotional glimpse of Jesus in deep agony, bawling at the tomb of his friend Lazarus. We see this same Jesus in Matt 26, earnestly pleading for release from the impending agony of his crucifixion. The healer of others is himself immersed in agony. Did Jesus consciously choose to run toward this pain instead of avoiding it? Perhaps this is his way of inviting us to understand that he fully shares in our sufferings, highlighting that the traumas we undergo should not be disregarded or suppressed through praise. To divorce Jesus from suffering is to overlook essential layers of his identity.

If therefore, Jesus, the embodiment of divinity, could bear the weight of trauma without suppressing his emotions, how much more should we, as humans, engage with our own experiences of trauma? I grew up in Antigua, a culture that lacked a healthy framework for processing or discussing traumas, including death and sexual abuse. We were often encouraged to swiftly "get over it" or, at the very least, avoid discussing it altogether. The prevailing belief was that speaking about pain would anchor it within us, while silence might diminish its presence. Yet, the harsh reality was that trauma remained a constant and destructive presence. Antigua is a nation that was colonized by the British and has its own history of oppression, long-term trauma, and marginalization. In hindsight, it appeared as if no one knew that they could permit themselves to grieve or express their pain using their own words.

In my religious Christian communities, the familiar billion-dollar questions still linger: "Why do bad things happen?" "What causes the tectonic plates in Haiti to trigger such devastation?" "How do we explain wildfires in California?" "Why are children born with debilitating diseases?" "What about the heart-wrenching reality of children dying before their parents?" Answers to these questions remain elusive, and there exists no predefined method to alleviate the anguish and uncertainty. This struggle is mirrored in the biblical texts themselves, as the writers grappled and fumbled with how to respond to suffering and evil.

Suffering and evil, whether in the form of natural disasters, accidents, or systemic injustices like racism, are ubiquitous aspects of existence. The Christian faith, grounded in the belief of a benevolent God, precludes the notion that these adversities are ordained by God. Consequently, the church should no longer participate in concealing these harsh realities. Instead, it is being summoned by those who suffer, including myself, to transform from a repository of shallow expressions into a platform where individuals can openly pen their narratives of pain, along with their existential questions of "Why?" This transformation is imperative.

In John 11, when Jesus intentionally arrived late is juxtaposed with him weeping over Lazarus's tomb. The more I think about this passage, the more I want to think about it. Why bother to weep when Lazarus would momentarily be made alive? The tears seem out of sync with the beginning and the end. It could be that the weeping is a revelation of Jesus' inner feelings. In addition, the resurrection theme that emerges in this story has communal tones. Lazarus's death was experienced by a community. Thus, his rising also had implications for the community.

Chapter 32

Trauma in Job

THE BOOK OF JOB is a rich plot characterized by great complexity. It revolves around a man whom God declares righteous but who subsequently experiences a relentless series of traumatic events—seemingly reserved for the unrighteous. Remarkably, this man was also prosperous, enjoying a life seemingly blessed with every imaginable fortune. However, this prosperity creates a conundrum, as in the context of the book, wealth and good health were tightly intertwined.

In this book, we find a family struck by what can be termed as "friendly fire." This is a dilemma that, let's admit, we are familiar with. We have witnessed it; some of us have lived it. It is the kind of quandary that keeps us awake at night, prompting us to question the existence of God or whether God cares for us at all. Such experiences can even push us away from God. I wonder if the biblical writers were conscious of the peril embedded in the story they narrated. This danger remains as real today as it was then. Whenever we confront hard questions, seek unvarnished truths, and reject facile answers, we wade into risky territory. The book of Job invites us to ask these demanding questions, confronts harsh realities, and provides a model for engaging in these challenging conversations. If there's any hopeful message to glean from this, it may be that God is capable of embracing our questions, our realities, and our uncomfortable truths.

Amid the intricate narrative of Job is his wife, a figure worth observing. In Job 2:9, while Job was defending his faith in the wake of his children's deaths and the loss of his wealth, she advises him to curse God and die. It's quite a statement!

"Do you still persist in your integrity?" In this context, the term "integrity" equates to piety. Mrs. Job is essentially asking her husband, "Why are you trying to maintain a facade of holiness while ignoring the grief you know caused by the deaths of your children? Why not speak the truth?" Her question is not a sign of her lacking faith; rather, it is she who emerges as the insightful one here. She urges Job to be honest with God and with himself. The question she poses is whether we grant ourselves the permission and space to express anger, confusion, or incomprehension to God. In her capacity as a grieving mother, she encourages her husband to shed the role of "Job the Righteous" and lean into "Job the Human Being." There are limits to our understanding of God, and in light of that, certain events may appear genuinely cruel, such as the death of a child.

Mrs. Job emerges as one of the most candid and courageous characters in the book. She should be recognized as a mother who carried, birthed, nurtured, and loved the very children whose deaths she encouraged Mr. Job to grieve. Instead, she is often vilified in Christian settings due to our perceptions of the "correct" way to respond to trauma. Perhaps this stems from our resistance to harsh truths or our insistence on the "right" way to grieve. Throughout history, some people have even cautioned their daughters against emulating her. I propose that we should indeed emulate her. We should adopt honesty, acknowledge our trauma, and work toward its transformation to prevent its perpetuation.

We owe this woman an apology. She has been cast aside from the narrative, her role marginalized and her experiences scorned for centuries. This dismissal mirrors a kind of societal rejection reminiscent of overturning *Roe v. Wade*. Mrs. Job's character, albeit briefly featured, serves as a symbol of the erasure of women's voices, perpetuated both by patriarchy and the tendency of some women to undermine each other.

The church tends to overshadow the kingdom of God with books authored by mortals. I appreciate the excitement that arises when we read of Job's restoration of wealth and the birth of new children. However, we must acknowledge the cruelty of overlooking the fact that no number of new children can replace the ones who perished. The essence of the story lies not in Job's eventual material prosperity but in God's presence. Even if God were to send the angel Gabriel to explain my own son's death, I doubt it would alleviate my grief. My son would still be gone, and therefore, my pain would persist.

Although the book of Job is not the Bible's opening book, it is often considered the oldest because it addresses the most ancient question in the world: "Why?" I find this book deeply unsettling, and that's precisely what draws me to it.

Early in the book, we discern that being called by God and serving faithfully do not exempt anyone from life's hardships. Christianity does not provide immunity against troubles. If one lives long enough, they will discover that the worst possible misfortune can befall anyone at any time. While the saying goes "While there is life, there is hope," I want to emphasize that along with life comes the possibility of pain. We will inflict pain on others, and others will inflict pain on us. Sometimes, it is intentional, while at other times, it is a result of ignorance. History attests that even when you stand on the right side in the right place, you can still be struck by friendly fire. The term "friendly fire" is somewhat lunatic in itself, yet apropos, for it is in the sanctuary too often, where one faces betrayal and harm. I believe Job can relate to this sentiment as he faced down his friends.

Chapter 33

THOUGH THE BOOK OF Job is a strange tale, it is also a philosophical exploration of various themes, unraveling intricate relationships, faith, and life's turbulent journey. Emotions surge throughout the narrative, shaping the experiences of its characters. Here is an examination of some of these themes through a broader lens.

Shock: The Jobs initially grappled with sheer shock as their lives took multiple tragic turns. They were thrust into circumstances beyond their control, leaving them bewildered and distressed. Similarly, though for different causes, Job's friends also experienced shock, which eventually transformed into accusations. When they shifted from offering support during the Jobs' distress to assigning blame and judgment, they intensified the family's anxiety.

Fear: The friends themselves likely harbored fear. Seeing the calamity that befell Job, they may have feared that a similar fate could befall them. In Antigua, we would say, "When your neighbor's house catches fire, wet yours." This fear is not unfounded, as the story demonstrates that no one is exempt from life's trials. The Jobs and subsequently their children may have also likely wrestled with fear when one calamity followed the next.

Anger: Unsurprisingly, anger permeates the narrative. The Jobs have every reason to be furious—at God, at their children, at their community, at their friends, at themselves, and at the entire world. The character of Job encapsulates the human experience of anger in the face of suffering. He is not afraid to express his raw, unfiltered emotions. His anger is directed at God, at the arbitrary nature of his misfortunes, and at his friends, who accuse him of wrongdoing. This anger, while unsettling, serves as a powerful reminder of the depth of human pain.

Similarly, the book portrays a complex interplay of blame, with Job's friends insinuating that his suffering must be a consequence of his sin. This blame-shifting illustrates how, when confronted with suffering, we may seek simple explanations or place responsibility on the afflicted individual rather than grappling with life's inherent complexities.

The undercurrent of hurt intensifies this anger, making it a potent emotional force. This anger is not synonymous with violence but can serve as a catalyst for change. Unless we feel some anger and hurt about acts of injustice, no action will be taken to bring about change. Anger can mobilize individuals and communities to confront injustice, demand accountability, and work toward a more just society. When appropriately channeled, it becomes a force for positive change, driving activism, advocacy, and community organizing.

Coping with anger in a healthy manner is paramount. This involves creating safe spaces for dialogue, seeking therapy or counseling, and engaging in life-giving practices. These can guide us toward a more just and compassionate world.

Hurt: Beneath the surface of these emotions lies overwhelming hurt. The Jobs' suffering, coupled with their friends' insensitivity, magnifies their pain. This deep-seated hurt is a central element that should not be overlooked.

Zooming in, we find Mr. Job expending considerable effort trying to convey to his friends that there is no rational explanation for the family's plight. It's intriguing to note that this occurs precisely when one needs a robust support system the most—when life takes a devastating turn. This is not the time for the afflicted individual to "be strong"; it's the time for the support system to fortify itself and provide unwavering assistance. Job required the support of his community, not accusations and rumors. However, in their ignorance and immaturity, Job's friends committed two unhelpful acts: they attempted to explain God to Job, and they placed blame on him. Furthermore, Mrs. Job faced backlash for expressing her authentic feelings about her children's deaths and the collapse of her life with her husband. Her expression disrupts the facades and head games we often engage in. Her courage shines through.

Sufferer-shaming is a recurring issue that can provoke anger. It is far too easy to judge from the outside, peering in through distorted lenses. Our fear of authenticity leads us to romanticize suffering as if it were a badge of honor, as if suffering inherently makes one holier. However, suffering is not a pathway to salvation in and of itself.

Mr. Job, in his interactions with unsupportive friends, refuses to accept their explanation that his family's suffering is directly tied to some sin he may have committed. His actions here are prophetic and liberating. He might have once shared his friends' perspective regarding the correlation between sin and suffering, but the tragic events he experiences challenge this paradigm. His children's deaths and the loss of his wealth become a transformative lens through which he views suffering and God. His body, afflicted with sores, becomes a tangible representation of his ordeal.

When Arleigh died, my skin also broke out. Job's failing health could have been caused by his body's response to grief. A familiar adage is that a person's health is their wealth. These days, this is truer than before. The cost of health care has forced some people to choose between paying for food, paying for shelter, or paying for their medicine.

Sin is not the cause for every problem. Though their expressions of it were different, Mr. and Mrs. Job recognized this. Mr. Job might have also discovered that there were many others who were suffering in similar ways as he was. Consequently, his arguments with his friends may have been a form of solidarity and advocacy. Since my son died, I have met many, many other mothers who are outliving children, and we have formed an organic solidarity. There's one whose daughter died after Arleigh did, who said to me, "Pastor, I understand now." She was later diagnosed with breast cancer and noted that since being diagnosed with breast cancer, she has met many other survivors, making her much more aware of her own mortality.

The words in Job 42:3–6 feel as if Mr. Job is acquiescing to a senselessly violent theodicy. Could he be repenting of his call for God to answer? He may be repenting, or he may be acknowledging the limits of his humanity. I personally prefer the latter. It is unlikely that Job betrayed his solidarity with other sufferers because the pain of a child's death is not one that can be salved with the birth of another. Job's new children did not replace those who died. Neither was Job's joy at the birth of the new children meant to be a replacement for his grief.

The Job family is a great example of how suffering and poverty can happen to even innocent people without clear explanation. It opens up questions concerning the intersection of God, evil, suffering, and how humans relate to them. Though the book does not offer any definitive answers, it is a way of "singing the Lord's song" in the strange land of suffering.

Chapter 34

God Says a Word

AFTER ALL THE HURT, fear, uncertainties, and angsts of the first thirty-seven chapters of the book, God says something to Job—instead of only about Job like in the bargain at the beginning. Is anybody else bothered by what God did in the beginning of the book?

I am also very interested in what God says to Job's friends. The response is a pivotal theological moment that addresses the complexities of divine justice, human suffering, and the limitations of human understanding. In this response the vast gulf between divine wisdom and human understanding is further underscored. The friends attempted to explain Job's suffering through a retributive justice framework, implying that his afflictions were punishments for sin. However, God's challenge to them, notably through the series of questions about the creation and ordering of the universe, highlights their limited understanding and misrepresentation of divine actions. This encounter emphasizes God's sovereignty and the mystery of God's ways, which transcend human logic and moral frameworks.

Job's friends represent a conventional theological stance that rigidly equates suffering with divine retribution. Their speeches to Job imply that righteousness should lead to prosperity and well-being, while suffering is indicative of sin and divine displeasure.

God's response criticizes this simplistic and transactional view of divine justice. It suggests a more complex and nuanced understanding of God's relationship with the world, where suffering is not always a direct result of individual sin.

In defending himself against the accusations of his friends, Job maintains his integrity and righteousness, challenging the notion that his suffering must be a punishment for sin. God's vindication of Job and rebuke of his friends affirm the legitimacy of Job's lament and protest. It shows that authentic relationship with God includes the freedom to express doubt, anguish, and incomprehension in the face of suffering. The religious community needs to honor this truth!

God's response to Job's friends serves as a call to humility in theological discourse. It warns against the arrogance of speaking for God or claiming comprehensive understanding of God's ways. The narrative invites readers to approach theology with humility, acknowledging the limits of human perspective and the mystery of divine providence.

Finally, God's response and the subsequent command for Job's friends to offer sacrifices and for Job to pray for them indicate the importance of solidarity and compassionate presence in the face of suffering. Rather than theological speculation or moral judgment, the preferred response to human suffering is one of empathy, support, and intercession.

Gustavo Gutiérrez posits that "what God is criticizing here is every theology that presumes to pigeonhole the divine action in history and gives the illusory impression of knowing it in advance."[1]

I firmly believe in the inherent goodness of God, yet this conviction should not lead us to overlook our human experience. Acknowledging God's goodness does not negate the dreadful realities we face, nor does it attribute such suffering to divine will. Sanctity does not inhibit our journey toward holistic healing; rather, it necessitates confronting the voids within our existence—our pain, anguish, trauma, and grief.

---

1. Gutiérrez, *On Job*, 72.

Echoing the experience of Job, we may not always find answers to our queries. However, this lack of resolution should not compel us to dismiss these questions. Authenticity in our emotional expression is paramount; God values our genuine anguish more highly than insincere adulation.

Indeed, God's response to Job's friends challenges overly simplistic and reductive theological explanations for suffering. It calls for a recognition of divine transcendence, the integrity of the sufferer, the virtue of theological humility, and the necessity of compassionate solidarity in the human encounter with suffering and mystery.

Chapter 35

*"God is it really quite alright to show you where it hurts?
How much sight do you have left?"* (Journal excerpt)

Lament and a Call to Smite in Psalm 137

RATHER THAN CONFRONTING OUR traumas, grief, and pain and establishing constructive mechanisms to process them, the Christian community often hastens individuals to adopt an appearance of fortitude, urging them to prioritize praise over the articulation of their suffering. This creates a scenario where genuine expression of pain is seemingly traded off for superficial exaltation, leading to a lack of space for "Holy Saturday" moments—times when the disruption of life's joy should be acknowledged. This approach risks aligning us with the perspective of Job's friends, who, confined by their dualistic view of divine justice, perceived Job's affliction as a dilemma to be rectified rather than an existential condition to be embraced and transformed. In this context, Ps 137 resonates with the solemn reflection required on such "Holy Saturdays," capturing the tumult of overwhelming distress.

The Psalms, predominantly categorized as lamentations, resonate with us for their authentic depiction of anguish and pleas for divine intervention. These texts articulate the complexities of human experience, offering a voice to the disarray and distress that often permeate our existence. Generations of Christians find solace in reciting the Psalms.

In the United Methodist Church hymnal, selected verses from the Psalms, including Ps 137, are featured. Despite the affinity many hold for these Psalms, there is a noticeable hesitation to incorporate them fully into worship practices. It seems that contemporary worship does not accommodate overt expressions of distress, such as the plea, "God, I am troubled and in trouble. Help me."

The emotional breadth of the Bible, encapsulated in the Psalms and extended throughout its narratives, spans a wide spectrum from anger and joy to sorrow and despair. This emotional diversity is evident in the lamentations of the psalmists, Jesus' emotional expressions in the Gospels, and the fear voiced by Elijah in the Old Testament. Given this rich culture of emotional expression, the question arises: Why does the church often fail to provide a nuanced response to the traumas afflicting our lives?

The Psalms served as the ancient hymnal, offering solace and expression to those in distress. Psalm 137, a poignant reflection on pain and alienation, though not traditionally classified among the lament Psalms, serves as a powerful vehicle for expressing the deep-seated agony associated with feelings of exile and loss. It provides a language for those grappling with the weighty sense of dislocation and disenfranchisement, enabling them to articulate the pain inherent in the feeling of not belonging. "By the rivers of Babylon . . ."

Psalm 137 dives into the trauma of a community exiled in Babylon, articulating the unfathomable suffering, pain, anger, grief, and despair of the people. The psalm captures the deep sense of alienation from their homeland and sacred spaces, reflecting the collective yearning for justice through its call for divine retribution against their oppressors, emblematic of an instinctual reaction to abstruse trauma.

Chapter 36

THE AFRICAN DIASPORA CAN resonate deeply with the sentiments of Ps 137, as it speaks to the historical experiences of displacement and enslavement. The psalm encapsulates the emotional turmoil inherent in the question, "How can we sing the Lord's song in a strange land?" (v. 4). This notion of a "strange land" becomes paradoxical when applied to the lived experiences of the African Diaspora, many of whom, including myself, have never yet physically visited Africa, "the Mother Land," yet harbor an intrinsic desire to connect with the ancestral soil under our feet and inhale the air that wafts through the trees carrying the stories of our history and heritage. For us, although we were born in lands outside of the continent of Africa, we are spiritually tied to the land where our ancestors were born.

Descendants of the enslaved and colonized peoples within the African Diaspora, notably in the United States and the Caribbean, often grapple with a sense of dislocation, even in their birthplaces. Their history is marked by narratives of abduction, exploitation, and systemic violence, which resonate with the themes of Ps 137. This psalm becomes a lens through which the ongoing struggles against state-sponsored violence and systemic oppression are viewed and understood.

The colonization of Antigua by the British serves as an example of such systemic disenfranchisement, where the local population was subjected to foreign domination, cultural suppression, and social marginalization without the benefits of British citizenship. This historical context highlights the paradox of colonial rule: governance without representation or rights.

Cheryl Sanders, in her book *Saints in Exile: The Holiness-Pentecostal Experience in African American Religion and Culture*, characterizes the African American experience as an "exilic dialectic," underscoring a pervasive sense of homelessness and alienation. This enduring disconnection is perpetuated through discriminatory practices like redlining and societal exclusion. Consequently, the African Diaspora continues to navigate the challenge of "singing the Lord's song in a strange land," confronting the reality of racial prejudice and exclusion in spaces often claimed exclusively by non-Blacks.

This exploration of Ps 137 through the experiences of the African Diaspora illuminates a broader narrative of displacement, resistance, and the quest for identity and belonging in a world that frequently reminds them of their historical and ongoing estrangement.

Chapter 37

IN THE CARIBBEAN, WHERE I originate, "Babylon" is a term used to denote systems of oppression, including the British-influenced police force. Bob Marley's anthem "Chant Down Babylon" reflects a deep-seated longing for a peaceful existence. N. S. Murrell highlights how Caribbean artists, particularly within the Rastafarian movement, have embraced lamentation as a form of resistance against the enduring scars of colonialism and slavery, manifesting in systemic oppression and poverty in regions like Jamaica.[1] This is encapsulated in the poignant echo of Ps 137, where the captivity and longing for Zion are lamented.

Rastafarians understand this biblical lament, yet historically, they have proactively sought to redefine their destiny, refusing to await deliverance from a deity perceived as complicit in their prolonged suffering. The lyrics of Bob Marley's "Buffalo Soldier" symbolize this active resistance, narrating the story of African individuals uprooted and thrust into perpetual struggle. "Chanting down Babylon" thus becomes an act of defiance and a transformative appropriation of lament, challenging oppressive structures.

The litany of adversities—ranging from personal tragedies, organizational disruptions, natural disasters, to systemic injustices—underscores the ubiquitous nature of suffering and the resultant necessity for lament. These experiences, reflected in the

---

1. Murrell, "Psalms."

modern-day echoes of Ps 137, underscore a collective and historical resonance with the themes of displacement and injustice.

The inquiry in Ps 137:4, "How shall we sing the Lord's song in a strange land?" captures the intense dissonance of attempting to harmonize faith with the experience of alienation. This contemplation challenges the traditional notions of worship and questions the inclusivity of lament within the spectrum of divine songs.

Worship should be therapeutic, embracing the full spectrum of human experience, allowing expressions of both jubilation and distress. However, there is often a marked disconnect between the potential for worship to facilitate healing and the actual practice within Christian communities. By neglecting the integral role of lament in worship, the church overlooks an essential aspect of communal and individual well-being.

Incorporating lament into worship not only bridges the gap between individual pain and communal support but also fosters a deeper, more authentic engagement with the divine. It transforms worship from a mere observance into an interactive space where vulnerability is honored, and collective healing can commence. Ignoring the role of lament in worship risks silencing a vital aspect of our spiritual expression, as poignantly warned in Ps 137:6, "may our tongues cling to the roofs of our mouths" if we fail to acknowledge and articulate our deepest sorrows.

Chapter 38

VERSES 8 AND 9 of Ps 137, with their stark imagery of retribution ("O daughter Babylon, you devastator! Happy shall they be who pay you back what you have done to us! Happy shall they be who take your little ones and dash them against the rock!"), present a moral and theological challenge, often perceived as a call for violence. One church leader expressed a desire to exclude these verses from the canon, aiming to "clean it up." Yet, these challenging verses resonate with the theme of divine justice seen in Rev 16, where God is depicted as delivering salvation while simultaneously destroying wickedness. Such passages underscore the biblical call for liberation from oppression and persecution, suggesting a divine imperative to eradicate such evils.

The visceral response evoked by Ps 137:9 mirrors my personal longing for divine retribution against the reckless actions that led to my son's death.

The decision by The United Methodist Church hymnal editors to include Ps 137 in full represents a commitment to acknowledging the pain of those affected by displacement and trauma. In times of recurring crises, it is apt to align our prayers with the psalmist, voicing the injustices of our time and seeking divine intervention against the forces of racism, war, and domination. This not only allows us to surrender our vengeful desires to God but also keeps us attuned to the necessity of combating evil.

Chapter 39

Psalm 137 is a captivating roller coaster of emotions that resonates with both the depth of grief and unsettling violence. While its jarring conclusion, which contemplates dashing infants against rocks, understandably shocks us, it is imperative that we confront this text head-on. Although certain portions of the psalm have been embraced through musical renditions, such as "Rivers of Babylon," these renditions often omit the unsettling aspects of the biblical version.

The Missing Conclusion: A Key to Understanding

Psalm 137 remains incomplete without considering its conclusion in verses 7–9. Neglecting this aspect diminishes the full spectrum of its poetic and political impact. By digging deeper into the historical and emotional context of this poem, we can begin to grasp the extreme struggles of the community that produced it.

Trauma and Theological Disorientation

To truly comprehend Ps 137, we must transport ourselves to the traumatized community of Judahites who composed it. These individuals had recently emerged from the throes of the Babylonian exile during the sixth century BCE. Before their exile, they harbored the belief that God would shield them from any invaders. However, the trauma of displacement, occupation, and theological disillusionment shattered this conviction.

The Yearning for Justice

The psalm's final verses, where the unsettling fantasy of infanticide resides, express a fervent desire for justice against Babylon, their merciless oppressor. Beyond the harsh words lies a great hope that the legacy of Babylonian violence would be severed entirely—an anguished plea for the cruelty to cease.

Empathizing with the Hurt

To engage with this psalm adequately, we must approach it with empathy, particularly when considering the traumatic backdrop and intricate power dynamics at play. It is essential to recognize that the oppressed community lacked the means to enact the violence described; instead, they entrusted the task of retribution to God and, perhaps, to the Persians, whom they envisioned as divine agents.

Rhetoric and the Language of the Unheard

The usage of violent rhetoric by marginalized communities, as exemplified in Ps 137, serves as a desperate cry for acknowledgment, humanity, and visibility when other avenues of expression prove futile. While the ethical implications of such rhetoric are multifaceted, it often represents a deep yearning for recognition, reverberating with the voices of the unheard. One of the great calypsonians in Antigua—The Monarch King Short Shirt—sang this in his seminal song "Not By Might."

Chapter 40

Moreover, Ps 137, along with the other passages explored in this work, serves as a narrative exploration of death, displacement, and the journey from desolation to restoration, highlighting the importance of recognizing and addressing trauma. The passages examined will be viewed through a lens of liberation and acknowledging the often-overlooked traumas within the narratives.

Thinking back on the period following my son's death, I realized that I felt a deep sense of spiritual and emotional dislocation, exacerbated by certain Christian perspectives that trivialized the tragedy. This led to a distancing from my spiritual roots, or "Zion," amid attempts to rationalize the loss with platitudes that "God knows best."

The book of Ruth also facilitates an understanding of the transition from displacement to re-placement, capturing the nuances of this journey. This insight is drawn from my desire for the Christian community to develop more effective ways of supporting individuals through prolonged periods of trauma, a necessity highlighted by the inadequate response of Job's friends and mirrored in my experience of community neglect following Arleigh's death. This lack of support deepened our sense of isolation and compounded our grief, casting us into a new form of "strange land," devoid of the communal solidarity I had previously provided to others in their times of distress.

PART 2: BIBLE TALK

In wrestling with the depth of my son Arleigh's death, I have rediscovered the therapeutic potency of lamentation. It serves as a crucial means of confronting, rather than disregarding, the realities of suffering, isolation, and malevolence. My work with the book of Ruth illuminated the depths of despair experienced by its female protagonists (Ruth, Naomi, and Orpah). Naomi's act of renaming herself struck a chord with me, mirroring the harrowing anguish I endure from the death of my son, encapsulating a strong expression of lament.

Chapter 41

> *The Book of Ruth is a short story about negotiating life's seasons. It catches up death, grief, loss, famine, life, recovery, survival, harvest, and hope.*
>
> —Andrea Campbell Byer Thomas, Teaching Tuesdays: About Ruth

Trauma and Displacement in the Book of Ruth

THE BOOK OF RUTH elevates often-silenced voices, challenging narratives that romanticize certain actions while neglecting the inherent dangers and injustices.

The biblical narrative is replete with tales that transition from adversity to redemption, resonating with the Christian community's penchant for celebrating triumphant resolutions. These narratives often encapsulate the biblical journey from despair to deliverance, epitomized by the account of Ruth and Boaz. My examination of this story is through a critical lens that probes into the pain and uncertainties typically glossed over.

The book of Ruth is characterized by its theme of displacement. Dr. Judy Fentress-Williams highlights the fluid position of Ruth within the Christian canon, noting its inclusion in the Megilloth, or festival scrolls, where its placement varies. When arranged by presumed date of authorship, Ruth precedes the others, while a liturgical sequence places it after the Song of Songs. In the Septuagint, the Greek rendition of the Old Testament, Ruth immediately follows Judges. This thematic versatility of Ruth, encompassing elements of famine and abundance, loss and redemption, as well as death, mourning, and renewal, underscores its enduring relevance and adaptability across different temporal and canonical contexts.[1]

The narrative of Ruth commences with a family's migration to Moab from Bethlehem, a city biblically emblematic as the "house of bread," which paradoxically is afflicted by famine at this juncture. The ensuing famine is a harbinger of death, with both elements intricately woven to depict a backdrop of desperation and deep loss.

Out of desperation, Elimelech, a man of the tribe of Judah and Naomi's husband, leaves his home in Bethlehem and heads to Moab. This could not have been an easy decision to make, considering the rift that existed between these two cousin groups of people: two neighboring countries of ancient Israel, to the east of the Jordan River and the Dead Sea, in what is today the kingdom of Jordan.

---

1. Fentress-Williams, *Ruth*, 10.

Chapter 42

THE BOOK OF RUTH narratively encapsulates the complexities of ethnic division and the ensuing journey of Elimelech's family, marked by deep-seated emotions and the harrowing reality of entering an unknown land. Their experience, characterized by sighs and groans, mirrors the contemporary journeys of immigrants moving to the United States, where the promise of reception remains uncertain. While many churches welcome these new members, providing pathways for assimilation, they often lack the mechanisms to address the traumas accompanying these individuals.

In the narrative arc of the book, the demise of Elimelech and his sons within a decade of their migration to Moab leaves Naomi as the sole survivor, prompting her lamentation of feeling bitterly treated by the Lord (Ruth 1:20). This expression of grief and the re-naming of herself as "Mara" signify the impact of her losses, underscoring the necessity of allowing individuals like Naomi the time and space to process their grief fully.

The root of *Shaddai* translates as "breast." Naomi's use of this in Ruth 1:20 offers a nuanced perspective of God, resonating with notions of nurture, fierce love, and sustenance. This depiction not only broadens the understanding of the Divine but also intersects with feminist theological interpretations.

Naomi's odyssey from Bethlehem to Moab, and her eventual return, encapsulates a spectrum of human experience, rich in its portrayal of loss, displacement, and the paradoxes of human existence. Departing Bethlehem, a city ironically named "house of bread," during a period of severe famine, Naomi embarks on a journey filled with hope and the presence of her loved ones. Her departure, spurred by the desperate search for sustenance, paradoxically occurs in a state of emotional "fullness." She is "full" because her familial bonds are intact; her husband and sons are by her side, embodying a sense of wholeness and security amid the scarcity that drives them from their homeland.

However, Naomi's narrative arc bends toward tragedy as Moab becomes less of a refuge and more a place of loss. The death of her husband and sons in this foreign land marks a harrowing transition from fullness to emptiness, a void that starkly contrasts with the physical fullness she left behind in Bethlehem. This poignant shift underscores a deeper existential crisis; the physical famine in Bethlehem pales in comparison to the emotional and spiritual famine she experiences in Moab.

She returns to Bethlehem to find that the city is no longer a place of famine but one of harvest and physical abundance. Yet, Naomi's declaration of emptiness upon her return, in the midst of this abundance, serves as a stark testament to the gut-wrenching losses she has endured. The physical satiety of Bethlehem's harvest cannot fill the gaping void left by her deceased family members. Her statement that she left "full" and returned "empty" is not about the material conditions but the emotional and relational bereavement that defines her experience felt at a visceral level.

Chapter 43

IN THIS LIGHT, NAOMI's journey between Bethlehem and Moab becomes a poignant exploration of the human condition, where physical realities and emotional experiences are deeply intertwined yet distinctly impactful. Her story is a raw and unvarnished depiction of the complexities of life, where the fullness of the heart can turn to emptiness, even as the barrenness of the land gives way to plenty. Through Naomi's eyes, we witness the harsh truth that the loss of loved ones leaves a void no amount of material abundance can repair, illustrating the often paradoxical nature of human suffering and resilience.

I deeply resonate with the narrative of loss and emptiness. My children, affectionately termed "The Fantastic Four," have been the essence of my being. One of them now enhances the celestial realm with his humor. His death has left an irreplaceable emptiness within me. Similarly, Naomi, despite the prospect of sustenance and the company of her daughter-in-law, confronts the grief that resides within her. She must navigate the solitude of her loss, underscoring the irreplaceable nature of human familial bonds, unmitigated by material provisions or any other substitutes. Naomi's experience resonates with my own, affirming the indelible impact of such loss.

This chronicle illuminates a distinct form of deprivation in Ruth 1: a deficit of human connection. Naomi's return perhaps was met with indifference or even disdain, accentuating her vulnerability as a widow bereft of male support, which was crucial in her cultural context. Her situation exemplifies a different dimension of famine—a famine of compassion and companionship.

This reflection propels us toward reconsidering the essence of our relationships, especially in light of recent years marked by pandemic-induced isolation, revealing the critical need for a shift in how we engage with one another. It serves as a reminder of the importance of fostering spaces where individuals can thrive and cultivate meaningful connections, regardless of life's vicissitudes. In the throes of death's desolation, it is the depth and health of human relationships that can partially mitigate the void, reinforcing the necessity of nurturing empathetic and supportive communal ties.

Chapter 44

Where you go, I will go; where you lodge, I will lodge; your people shall be my people, and your God my God.
—Ruth 1:16b

Following Elimelech's death, Naomi finds herself as a widow and single mother in unfamiliar surroundings. The exact nature of Naomi's challenges in this foreign land remains undisclosed, yet, from my own experience as a single parent abroad, the difficulties are often overwhelming. Naomi likely found herself compelled to persevere, driven by the same dire needs that initially led her family to migrate, reminiscent of Jacob's family seeking sustenance in Egypt. Yet, in contrast to Joseph's extended lineage, Elimelech and his sons succumbed shortly after their relocation (Ruth 1:14). This loss naturally inclined Naomi toward returning to her native land, possibly to partake in rituals aiding in her mourning process.

The story unfolds with her daughters-in-law expressing intentions to accompany her, highlighting the close bonds formed, transcending mere familial ties. Their offer, laden with grief and potential disorientation, underscores a shared bereavement and the daunting prospect of a new displacement.

The deaths of their husbands introduce a significant existential crisis, mirroring Naomi's loss. The scriptural silence on the cause of their demise evokes personal reflections on my son's death, where the intrusive curiosity of others about the circumstances compounded the grief. Such experiences emphasize the necessity of reevaluating our approach to interpreting and reacting to others' suffering to avoid inflicting further pain. The immediate need in such sorrowful times is compassionate companionship, embodying the enduring presence in the shadow of grief as depicted in Ps 23.

Among the daughters-in-law, Orpah opts to remain in her homeland, possibly seeking solace among her kin (Ruth 1:14), while Ruth embarks on a precarious journey with Naomi to a previously famine-stricken land. This decision introduces layers of uncertainty atop their shared grief. Ruth's decision, fueled by affection and loyalty, signifies a remarkable bond with Naomi, bridging historical animosities and facing the vulnerability of traversing conflict-ridden landscapes without male protection. Ruth's potential separation from her own mother further accentuates her vulnerability, as she and Naomi navigate a path fraught with challenges and tensions.

Upon Ruth and Naomi's arrival in Bethlehem, the town is abuzz with curiosity and speculation (Ruth 1:19). Ruth finds herself the center of attention, navigating a complex web of social dynamics. The "stirring" in the town raises questions about the locals' perception of Ruth as an outsider. Are they wary of her foreign identity, suspecting her intentions, or concerned about potential disruptions she might bring?

Chapter 45

MIGRATION OFTEN UNDERSCORES THE fragile nature of human relationships and societal norms. The arrival of non-locals can unsettle local communities, revealing underlying tensions and prejudices. While the narrative does not explicitly detail the reactions of the Moabites to Naomi's initial arrival, or the Bethlehemites to her return with Ruth, it is plausible to infer a mutual sense of unease and curiosity.

Ruth, now in Israelite territory, faces the challenge of navigating cultural stereotypes, particularly the stigmatized view of Moabites as licentious, stemming from historical narratives that link them to idolatrous practices (Num 25:1–5; 1 Kgs 11:1–8). This sexualization and demonization of foreign women, often perpetuated to justify their subjugation, echo broader themes of racial and ethnic discrimination.

Women of color, in particular, may resonate with the experience of being mischaracterized in ways that foster mistreatment and misunderstanding. Such stereotypes are not grounded in fact but serve as oppressive narratives to maintain dominance over women and foreigners. Ruth, amid these complexities, must also contend with the uncertainty of Naomi's allegiance once back in her homeland.

Boaz emerges as a pivotal figure, utilizing his status and resources to facilitate Ruth's integration, albeit with nuances of vulnerability and potential ulterior motives that the narrative later unfolds. This development introduces a multifaceted perspective on power dynamics, hospitality, and the negotiation of identity in a context marked by cultural and personal transitions.

Chapter 46

> *Many of us see ourselves as strangers in this world on our way to eternal life. . . . For this reason, we identify with strangers and include them in our journey. The stranger comes to teach us and give us a priceless gift—the gift of identity.*
>
> —Joan M. Marusken, United Methodist Women's Study on Immigration and the Bible

Finding Ruth: From Displacement to Re-placement

Ruth's narrative prominently identifies her as an immigrant, consistently labeled as "Ruth the Moabite" or "the one who returned with Naomi from Moab." This recurrent identification underscores her status as an outsider, a fact that the narrative structure relentlessly emphasizes. The crafters of the narrative would not let her live down whatever shameful origin story they weaved into her. Nonetheless, despite the hurdles she faces, Ruth's story eventually shifts toward a trajectory of potential redemption.

The introduction of Boaz, a relative of Naomi, marks a significant turn in Ruth's journey. The term *gibor* used to describe him suggests that he is a relative of considerable standing and influence within the community. Boaz's decision to address Ruth as "daughter" rather than focusing on her foreign status symbolizes a pivotal moment, inviting a reevaluation of her identity and encouraging others to perceive her beyond her ethnic background. Boaz, identified as a *gibor*, a term often associated with warrior-like valor, also acknowledges Ruth with the term *chayil* (Ruth 3:11), traditionally reserved for men, thereby recognizing her strength and character.

The act of naming carries substantial weight, serving as a powerful tool for defining and asserting identity. Dr. Wil Gafney's insights on naming emphasize its capacity to shape reality and confer agency. Historically, the act of naming has been wielded by colonizers to assert dominance, erasing indigenous languages, names, and cultural identities to enforce their own. In this context, Boaz's reference to Ruth as "daughter" significantly alters the narrative direction of her life.[1]

Ruth's story, marked by adversity and displacement, showcases her resilience as she navigates through unfamiliar territories and cultural landscapes, bearing the weight of her people's stigmatized history. Boaz's actions toward Ruth signify a transformative re-narration of her life, offering her a new pathway to redefine her identity beyond her painful experiences and heritage.

In Boaz's acknowledgment of Ruth's strength and past, he becomes a figure of redemption, restoring her sense of agency and dignity. His ability to perceive her courage and vulnerability signifies a mutual recognition of valor, where Ruth's openness about her scars allows Boaz to align his strengths with hers, forging a partnership of mutual respect and understanding. This narrative invites reflection on the often-expressed demand for strength in the face of loss, hinting at the need for a respite and acknowledgment of the enduring strength displayed by Ruth, Naomi, and Orpah in their shared trials.

In the narrative of the book of Ruth, Ruth appears to navigate her life under the influence or authority of Naomi. Old Testament scholar Dr. Wil Gafney raises the possibility that Naomi could have exploited Ruth for personal advantage.[2] Ruth's struggle to bal-

---

1. Gafney, *Woman's Midrash*, 38.
2. Gafney, *Women's Lectionary*, 219.

ance her personal identity with the societal expectations is evident throughout the text. Her impassioned plea to Naomi, as recorded in Ruth 1:16–17, might hint at a power dynamic where Naomi holds significant influence or control over her.

Ruth's life is marked by adversity, including poverty, unemployment, and the loss of her personal and national identity. The process of migration often leads to a transformation of self-perception and behavior, as individuals adapt to the customs and practices of their new environment. Ruth's gradual assimilation into Israelite society, culminating in the practice of levirate marriage, suggests a significant shift in her self-concept.

There is also an undercurrent of Ruth potentially bearing undue responsibility, perhaps even being blamed by Naomi for her son's death, adding a complex layer of guilt to her mourning. Naomi's strategies, especially as they pertain to Ruth's body and choices (Ruth 3:3–5), point to a deeper manipulation of Ruth's circumstances for Naomi's ends. However, Boaz's intervention signifies a pivotal change in Ruth's narrative.

Beyond personal struggles, Ruth likely faced societal and cultural discrimination due to her Moabite heritage and foreign status, which could have exposed her to additional risks and biases. Boaz's protective stance might also be seen as a shield against potential sexual exploitation. Ruth, young and widowed, navigating a new cultural landscape, embodies the vulnerabilities that could easily align her story with the narratives emerging from the #MeToo movement's focus on the vulnerability of women, particularly those marginalized by race, nationality, or socioeconomic status. While Boaz's actions are commendable, they also open up inquiries into the complexities of their relational dynamics.

The predicament of foreign women working as domestic helpers in the US and elsewhere, vulnerable to sexual predation and exploitation, echoes Ruth's potential plight. The societal and legal mechanisms, such as those in Lev 19:9–10, provide a framework for protection and provision, yet without active enforcement and empathetic intervention, individuals like Ruth remain at risk of falling through the cracks of the societal safety net.

Thanks to Boaz's actions, which surpassed the legal requirements, Ruth was able to preserve her dignity and humanity amid unfamiliar surroundings. At America's borders, numerous individuals, including women, children, and men, are attempting to reshape their narratives while seeking asylum and a more favorable existence. Unfortunately, the current legal framework often falls short in providing the necessary protection and provision for them, reminiscent of the biblical provision of gleaning. This legal inadequacy contributes to the re-traumatization of individuals who have already endured significant losses and are striving merely to survive, echoing the historical actions of those who established these laws long ago.

In Ruth's narrative transformation, Boaz is acclaimed as a man of valor (Ruth 2:1), a recognition attributed not to martial prowess but to his empathy and fundamental human kindness, demonstrating his readiness to extend beyond the minimal legal expectations. Reflecting on personal experiences, my husband, in his courtship, expressed a desire to be my Boaz, viewing the book of Ruth with a romantic perspective while acknowledging the harsher realities I had faced and his willingness to contribute positively to my life's journey.

The quest for agency leading to healing prompts a reflection on our capacity to acknowledge the traumas experienced by others and to integrate expressions of sorrow into our worship, enhancing divine movement in our lives and those observing our example. Recognizing and addressing the suffering of others not only facilitates healing but also fosters a more compassionate and responsive community, embodying the virtues of empathy and support illustrated by Boaz in the book of Ruth.

Chapter 47

And What If? Other Ways It Could Have Gone Down

WHAT IF THERE WAS more to the relational dynamics of Ruth and Boaz than the often-romanticized version? As a Moabite widow, Ruth occupies a precarious social position. Remember: She is a foreigner in Bethlehem, a land that historically harbors animosity toward her people. Naomi's return to Bethlehem with Ruth is marked by desperation, as both women are bereft of male protection and economic stability. Ruth's survival hinges on her ability to navigate these hostile and uncertain conditions.

The gleaning laws of ancient Israel, designed to provide for the poor and the foreigner, place Ruth in a position where she must depend on the kindness of landowners. Boaz, a wealthy and influential man in Bethlehem, emerges as her benefactor. While Boaz's actions are often viewed as noble, we must interrogate the power imbalance inherent in their relationship. Boaz's position of authority and Ruth's desperation create a dynamic ripe for exploitation.

Boaz's Power and Ruth's Vulnerability

Boaz's initial encounter with Ruth occurs in his fields, where she is gleaning. The text describes him as a "man of standing" (Ruth 2:1), a term that implies both wealth and influence. His first words to Ruth, recorded in Ruth 2:8–9, are often read as protective:

"Listen to me, my daughter. Don't go and glean in another field and don't go away from here. Stay here with the women who work for me. Watch the field where the men are harvesting and follow along after the women. I have told the men not to lay a hand on you. And whenever you are thirsty, go and get a drink from the water jars the men have filled."

While these instructions can be interpreted as caring, they also establish a controlling dynamic. Boaz's directive confines Ruth to his field, effectively isolating her from potential alternative sources of support. His insistence that she stay and glean only in his field can be seen as a means to assert control over her movements and access to resources. Furthermore, his assurance that the men will not harm her subtly underscores the inherent threat of sexual violence in her situation, a threat from which Boaz positions himself as her protector.

Chapter 48

The Threshing Floor Incident

THE STORY REACHES A pivotal and controversial moment on the threshing floor. Naomi instructs Ruth to wash, perfume herself, and put on her best clothes before going to meet Boaz secretly at night (Ruth 3:3–4). Naomi's advice to Ruth to uncover Boaz's feet and lie down is laden with sexual innuendo. The term "feet" in Hebrew is often a euphemism for genitalia, suggesting a possible sexual encounter.

Boaz, waking to find Ruth at his feet, reacts with a mixture of surprise and acceptance. His response, "Who are you?" (Ruth 3:9), indicates his initial confusion. Ruth's reply, "I am Ruth, your servant; spread your cloak over your servant, for you are next-of-kin," is a bold request for protection and marriage. Yet, this moment raises significant ethical concerns. Ruth is in a vulnerable position, following Naomi's strategic yet risky plan. Boaz's decision to honor her request can be seen as a commendable act of kindness, but it is also essential to question whether Ruth genuinely had the freedom to decline or negotiate under such circumstances.

The Ethics of Boaz's Actions

Boaz's subsequent actions, ensuring that Ruth leaves the threshing floor before dawn and providing her with six measures of barley (Ruth 3:14–15), may appear generous. However, these actions also serve to protect his reputation and maintain the secrecy of their encounter. By sending Ruth away before daylight, Boaz avoids potential scandal and preserves his status within the community.

The text does not provide explicit details about the nature of the encounter on the threshing floor, leaving room for speculation. If we consider the possibility of Boaz taking advantage of Ruth's vulnerability, his actions could be construed as coercive. Ruth's dependence on Boaz for survival and protection complicates the power dynamics at play. Boaz's ability to provide for Ruth places her in a position where refusal is not a viable option, highlighting the potential for exploitation.

Reassessing Redemption

The traditional interpretation of Boaz as a redeemer who rescues Ruth from her plight must be reexamined in light of these power dynamics. While Boaz's marriage to Ruth secures her future and integrates her into the Israelite community, it also reinforces his dominance and control over her. Ruth's agency is continually mediated through the actions and decisions of the men around her, from Naomi's strategic planning to Boaz's ultimate authority.

Furthermore, Boaz's willingness to marry Ruth is framed within the context of levirate marriage, a practice designed to preserve lineage and property within a family. His decision is influenced by social and economic considerations, rather than purely altruistic motives. The transaction-like nature of their union underscores the systemic subjugation of women within the patriarchal structure of ancient Israel.

Implications for Contemporary Readings

Examining Ruth and Boaz's relationship through the lens of sexual misconduct and power dynamics challenges us to confront uncomfortable truths about biblical narratives and their interpretations. It compels us to acknowledge the potential for exploitation within relationships marked by significant power imbalances.

For contemporary faith communities, this critical analysis serves as a call to vigilance against romanticizing or oversimplifying complex narratives. It underscores the importance of advocating for the vulnerable and scrutinizing the motivations and actions of those in positions of power. In doing so, we honor the spirit of the text by engaging with it honestly and seeking justice for those who, like Ruth, navigate precarious circumstances.

Chapter 49

Reflection and Notes on Forced Migration

JUST FOR A MOMENT, step into the shoes of those who have experienced forced migration and imagine leaving everything behind—not by choice but by necessity. What would you carry with you? What would you be forced to leave behind? When working with this reflection, consider the trinity of the physical, emotional, and spiritual implications of such a journey.

Some Helpful Questions to Guide This Reflection

- If you had to leave your home suddenly, what are the tangible things you would lose? Think beyond material possessions to aspects of your daily life that you value.
- Consider the intangible losses: relationships, community connections, a sense of belonging. How would these losses affect you?
- Forced migration often involves a loss of rights and agency. How would you cope with a situation where your choices are limited and your voice is not heard?
- Reflect on the cultural aspects—language, customs, traditions. How would the loss of these parts of your identity impact your sense of self?

- Lastly, consider the psychological impact. What are the emotional costs of being uprooted from your familiar environment and thrust into the unknown?

Consider some parallels between the literary themes of ancient Judaism, particularly those found in the book of Revelation, and contemporary narratives of immigration. Though the connection may not seem immediately apparent in the context of the twenty-first century, deeper thinking reveals similarities. Picture the journey of immigrants traversing diverse cultural landscapes, much like the historical migrations of peoples. They arrive filled with aspirations, carrying the "American Dream" in their hearts—a vision that closely mirrors the utopian ideals often described in apocalyptic literature.

The book of Revelation speaks of a New Jerusalem, a metaphor that has been adopted in American rhetoric to symbolize a land of opportunity and renewal. This imagery speaks to the transformative hopes that fuel the immigrant experience: the pursuit of a "better state" that has been whispered about and longed for. Yet, this same scriptural text (Rev 21–22), with its vision of renewal, also introduces a lexicon of exclusion—defining those who may enter and those who may not.

This duality echoes in contemporary debates about national identity and belonging in the United States. The language of Revelation has been co-opted in political discourse, shaping perceptions of America as a promised land while simultaneously delineating the contours of who is deemed worthy of inclusion within its borders. This selective position raises critical questions about the ethics of exclusion in a society that, at its core, is deeply rooted in the immigrant experience.

The metaphor of a "city on a hill" has resonated through American rhetoric for generations, originating from the Sermon on the Mount in the Gospel according to Matthew. This imagery, which is laden with eschatological undertones, serves as an archetype for an exemplary and luminous city, with Jerusalem traditionally interpreted as this exemplary city within the text. Intriguingly, President Ronald Reagan, in his valedictory address, revisited this metaphor, a motif frequently woven into his oratory. Reagan's portrayal of this city was vivid and robust, mirroring the grandeur and inclusivity described in Rev 21. He envisioned it as a "tall, proud city built on rocks stronger than oceans, wind-swept, and home to a diverse people living in concord."[1] In his articulation, the city—if it must be contained by walls—boasts gates that remain welcomingly ajar. This parallels the vision of the New Jerusalem in Revelation, a city with unyielding foundations named for the twelve apostles, with nations flowing into its brilliance, its gates perpetually open, inviting kings to tread its streets in continuous daylight. Such references underscore the deeply interwoven nature of biblical imagery and American civic identity, as articulated through presidential discourse.

---

1. Reagan, "Farewell Address."

Chapter 50

Some Costs and Effects of Forced Migration

Displacement from Sense of Home

HOME REPRESENTS A FOUNDATIONAL concept within the human experience. It is within this domain that our earliest memories are formed, our cultural norms are established, and our sense of security is rooted. The narrative of forced migration begins with a rupture in this primary relationship between individual and place. The biblical saga is replete with such ruptures—from the exile of Eden to the Babylonian captivity, these stories highlight the profound psychological and spiritual dislocation that accompanies physical displacement. The sense of nostalgia for the homeland, depicted in Psalms as the yearning for Zion by the waters of Babylon, reflects a deep-seated longing for the familiar and the sacred. Think about how this severance from home impacts identity and well-being and resonates with the millions today who find themselves refugees and asylum seekers.

Loss of Rights and Agency

Moving to the dynamics of rights and agency, the biblical paradigm of the *goy* and *ger* provides a rich tapestry for understanding the experiences of migrants. These categories capture the complexities of social inclusion and exclusion, as well as the transitions from being part of a majority to becoming marginalized. The *ger* often lives on the periphery of society, dependent on the protective laws and the hospitality of others, yet without full membership in the community. We find this paralleled in the modern struggle of stateless individuals and undocumented migrants. Their journey challenges us to reflect on the moral and ethical dimensions of citizenship and human rights. What does it mean to be a community of faith in light of these realities, and how do we respond to the loss of agency that so many endure?

Forced Assimilation and Loss of Identity

Assimilation is a multifaceted process, one that can lead to enriching multicultural societies but can also result in the erosion of distinct cultural identities. The forced assimilation of migrants can strip them of their languages, traditions, and cultural expressions. The biblical characters who faced the challenge of maintaining identity in the diaspora—such as Daniel in Babylon and Esther in Persia—demonstrate both resistance and accommodation to the dominant culture. These stories invite us to consider the price of assimilation and the resistance to cultural erasure. The conversation will broaden to contemporary experiences of migrants who negotiate their identities amid the pressures of integration, exploring the delicate dance between adaptation and the preservation of one's heritage.

Impulse to Exclude Others

The post-exilic community of Israel is an excellent case study of the impulse to exclude others. In Ezra 9–10, following the Babylonian captivity, the returnees to Jerusalem face a crisis of identity and faith, as many Israelite men have married foreign women. This intermingling is presented not just as a matter of cultural assimilation but as a violation of the covenant with God, risking the community's distinctiveness and its relationship with God.

Ezra, as a priest and scribe, perceives these marriages as a direct threat to the sanctity and survival of the nation. In a display of anguish, he prays and confesses the sins of the people, dramatically articulating the fear that such intermingling could dilute or even erase the hard-won identity of the Israelites. The solution enacted is a painful and controversial one: the community decides to dissolve these marriages and expel the foreign wives and their offspring. This decision is not without significant cost—families are torn apart, and the suffering is palpable. Doesn't this sound familiar in many tones? Yes, or yes?

This narrative is filled with complexity and ethical tension. On the one hand, there's a clear drive to maintain religious and cultural purity after a period of exile and trauma. On the other hand, the measures taken raise some moral questions, especially when viewed through a modern lens that values inclusivity and condemns forced separation.

In thinking through these passages, it is essential to consider the broader scriptural emphasis on justice, mercy, and the love of the stranger (*ger*). See what I did there? The *ger*, the sojourner or foreigner living among the Israelites, is repeatedly mentioned in the Hebrew Scriptures as one to be loved and protected. This command seems to stand in tension or even stark contrast with the actions taken in Ezra, suggesting that the community's response, while understandable in its historical context, presents a challenging precedent when considering modern issues of immigration and integration.

In considering the lessons from Ezra 9–10, we must ask ourselves: Can the drive for communal purity ever justify "othering" or the exclusion and mistreatment of the one from whom you are different? How do we balance the legitimate desire for cultural preservation with the imperative to act justly and love mercy, as the prophet Micah enjoins?

This conversation invites us to engage with the text not only as an ancient document but as a living dialogue that compels us to consider the implications of our actions on the vulnerable and the foreigner among us. In a world where migration and displacement continue to be pressing realities, the book of Ezra challenges us to confront these issues with both empathy and a critical eye toward the potential costs of prioritizing homogeneity over hospitality and human dignity.

We must also wonder about what it means when the "greeter" becomes the "gatekeeper"—when people who have experienced radical welcome turn around and decide that they are the only ones deserving or worthy of being in the region. Examining forced migration through the lens of Scripture and modernity calls us to a heightened awareness of the human cost associated with such displacement. It beckons us to a place of empathy and action, where we might consider our shared responsibility toward the stranger, the exile, and the refugee. When we reflect on these narratives, both ancient and contemporary, I hope that we find the wisdom to shape communities that uphold the dignity of every individual, honor the diversity of cultures, and foster justice and peace in a world that is too often marred by division and displacement.

Chapter 51

Addressing Divine Accountability in Joel 2:23–27

BIBLICAL TEXTS CAN BE read, heard, and interpreted in multiple ways. Misinterpretations, especially out of context, are of significant concern to me. The book of Joel, for instance, has been subject to such misreadings, with verses like "rend your heart and not your garments" often misrepresented or misquoted.

In my two decades of preaching, including numerous funerals and memorial services, I have consistently faced the paradox of celebrating life while mourning premature deaths. This dichotomy extends to recognizing God's protection yet grappling with the instances of seeming divine non-intervention in human suffering. It's an oversimplification to attribute all misfortunes to demonic forces, for such explanations bypass the complexity of these experiences.

We must acknowledge the mixed feelings of gratitude and sorrow that life's injustices provoke. The prevalence of societal and personal tragedies, from mass shootings, mass incarceration of Black and Brown people, famine, poisoned water, the loss of jobs and job security, divorce, the rise in home insecurity and homelessness, to personal losses, challenges us to broaden our understanding and empathy. In this light, I aim to focus on a less-discussed verse in Joel 2, which is often overlooked or superficially treated.

Joel 2:25 presents a thought-provoking message where the prophet conveys God's admission of sending the locusts, with God explicitly stating, "I did that." This acknowledgment compels us to confront the unsettling reality that the source of our pain might not always be external or malevolent forces but can also be divine orchestration or human decisions.

While the promise of restoration in Joel is uplifting, offering visions of abundant recovery and prosperity, it raises heavy questions about the nature of divine providence. The assurance of compensation for years lost to adversity is comforting, yet it begs the inquiry: Why allow the loss in the first place? This question challenges us to engage with the complexities of divine justice and the purpose behind both the infliction and the healing of suffering.

Chapter 52

SO, HOW DO WE respond when God permits our adversities? My thoughts often linger on the centuries-long slave trade and its modern iterations, the persistent injustices faced by people of color, and the systemic undervaluation and undercompensating of equally and sometimes more qualified women. Echoing the psalmist's lament, I find myself questioning, "How long, Lord? Will you forget your people forever?" This inquiry deepens when contemplating the divine promises that seem distant due to our enduring suffering.

My faith has never tolerated the superficial Christian doctrine that prohibits questioning God. To me, such an ideology breeds ignorance and fear. In thinking on Dietrich Bonhoeffer's notion of the "gnawing gap" that undeniably exists, I keep asking, "Why, God? Why?"[1] I am curious about why God allows certain events, and I find prompts for this inquiry within the Scripture itself. The act of recalling past blessings and anticipating future hope is vital. Scriptures like "rejoice . . . [because God] has given the early rain for your vindication" (Joel 2:23) and "You shall eat in plenty and be satisfied. . . . My people shall never again be put to shame" (Joel 2:26) do encourage us to acknowledge the continuity of God's goodness.

I recognize the good in my past and anticipate the good in my future, yet I currently reside in the challenging in-between,

---

1. Bonhoeffer, *Testament to Freedom*, 349.

where such recollections and anticipations are not readily accessible. In this state, I rigorously examine God's track record, not from a place of sanctity that claims to know all the answers, but from a position of bold inquiry, refusing to shy away from the necessary questions. Before embracing the promise of a better tomorrow, I must confront the realities of my present, albeit with glimpses of divine foresight offered by God.

While we might desire to evade the harsh truths of our existence and the questions they evoke, reality dictates otherwise. Only in sitcoms, like *Keeping Up Appearances* and the character of Hyacinth Bucket, do characters get rewarded for maintaining facades. If God acknowledges causing events like the locust plague, then perhaps this admission invites us to engage in open dialogue with God, even to question. This interaction forms a crucial part of wrestling with our faith and understanding amid life's complexities.

Chapter 53

Understanding the Trauma of Injustice Through Biblical Narratives

The Rape of Tamar in 2 Samuel 13

THIS IS AN EXAMPLE of how personal injustice can lead to emotional and psychological trauma, not only for the victim but also for the family and community involved. It is critical to our work as students of the Bible to spend time treating these passages in our communities because our communities hold some sway in how people locate themselves in the biblical narrative and how people see God in the realities of their lives. It is particularly troubling and apropos to talk about the rape of Tamar in this age because women and girls continue to be targeted by predominantly male legislators who restrict us from making reproductive and medical health care choices for ourselves. It is important to talk about how the female body has been co-opted even in the Scriptures and how it makes God out to be a common pimp, devaluing the lives of women and girls.

The text talks about Tamar's beauty and her brother Amnon's love for her. What he did as a result of this so-called love is not demonstrative of the healing that love generally brings. As a matter of fact, rape and other forms of abuse are incompatible with love.

While he feigned sickness acting up like a pregnant woman with cravings, and Tamar busied herself with the food preparation and cooking, he was able to lie there and watch her, leerily observing the movement of her body, practically stripping her with his eyes. That is an assault on her.

Tamar's Voice and Silence

At the core of 2 Sam 13 where Tamar's story lies, is an embodiment of both grace and tragic defeat. Her initial vibrant protests against her brother Amnon's intentions are heartbreakingly subdued, culminating in a deafening silence that echoes the historical suppression of women's voices. The move from vocal resistance to enforced quietude reflects Tamar's personal devastation and symbolizes the collective muting of women subjected to patriarchal dominance. This story implores us to recognize and challenge the enduring structures that perpetuate such oppression.

The silencing of Tamar's voice serves as a poignant example of a broader historical pattern where women's voices have been systematically muted within patriarchal societies. This phenomenon extends beyond individual instances of silencing to widespread cultural and institutional practice. It is evident in various forms, such as the legal and societal restrictions placed on women's rights, the exclusion of women from decision-making processes, and the often-dismissed or undermined reports of gender-based violence. This historical silencing not only affects the visibility of women's experiences but also perpetuates a cycle where the female perspective is continuously marginalized, impacting everything from legislation to everyday interactions.

Chapter 54

Interpreting Tamar Across Boundaries

EXPLORING TAMAR'S STORY THROUGH diverse cultural lenses illuminates its universal themes and the transformative power of Scripture when engaged by varied interpretative communities. This method enriches our comprehension and appreciation of the narrative, creating a vibrant dialogue space that honors every participant's voice. This story is perceived differently across cultural landscapes, reflecting varying societal values and norms. In some cultures, her story may be seen as a tragic tale of victimhood, while in others, it could be interpreted as a narrative of resistance against oppression. These interpretations are shaped by cultural attitudes toward gender roles, justice, and familial honor. For example, in collectivist societies, the emphasis might be on the family's honor and the shame brought upon it, whereas in more individualistic societies, the focus might be on personal agency and rights. It is within this confluence of interpretations that Tamar's ordeal is more fully understood, urging us to be attentive to the complex, layered essence of her experience and the broader implications for justice, redemption, and even resilience.

PART 2: BIBLE TALK

The Language of Tamar's Reality

The language used in Tamar's story is quite descriptive and serves as a powerful tool that shapes the reader's emotional and cognitive engagement with the story. The text employs rich metaphorical language that vividly portrays the intensity of Tamar's plight, embedding the themes of desire, violation, and resistance within its very structure. By digging deeper into this linguistic depth, we uncover multiple layers of meaning that resonate with the narrative's more dangerous and complex themes. The use of language and metaphors goes beyond a retelling to actively shape the reader's perception of the events. Language constructs reality and can either illuminate or obscure our understanding of trauma. Metaphors, in particular, serve as powerful tools that encapsulate complex emotions and situations in relatable terms, enabling readers to connect with Tamar's plight on a deeper level. For instance, describing her silence as a "stifled cry" or "muted echo" conveys the act of being silenced and the ongoing resonance of her voice despite this suppression. This linguistic crafting invites readers to explore the underlying emotions and societal implications of her story. Tamar's roar could be heard in her wearing of sackcloth and ashes.

A Psychoanalytic Exploration

A psychoanalytic exploration of Tamar's narrative reveals the deep psychological wounds inflicted both on her and on the community witnessing her degradation. This perspective allows us to empathize with her extreme suffering and challenges us to confront the harsh realities of such violence. By understanding the psychological dynamics at play, we can better address the trauma and possibly forge paths toward collective healing and empathy for those affected by similar traumas. This lens provides a depth of insight into the psychological impact of her trauma. Through this lens, we may be able to see the conflict between Tamar's own self-perception and the external forces imposing silence and shame upon her.

Psychoanalysis helps in understanding the long-lasting effects of such trauma, which may manifest as internal conflicts, altered self-image, and difficulties in trust and future relationships. Versions of Tamar are prevalent in our society, homes, and churches, and when the Tamars are silenced, whether willingly or unwillingly, communities are generally negatively affected. If we give attention to these dimensions, we can gain deeper empathy for Tamar and a broader understanding of how traumatic experiences can shape an individual's psyche over time.

Chapter 55

Historical Echoes: Tamar in the Annals of Time

POSITIONING TAMAR'S STORY WITHIN the broader historical and societal context reveals how power dynamics and moral corruption have perennially shaped human destinies. This historical perspective sheds light on the cyclic nature of such narratives and offers crucial lessons on the impacts of power misuse. It compels us to think about our current societal structures and the imperative to act decisively to amend the injustices that echo through time. The historical context provides critical insights into the cycles of power and exploitation that have pervaded societies across eras. These cycles manifest through the recurring themes of control over the vulnerable, the misuse of power by those in authority, and the societal complicity in silencing the oppressed. When we think about this, we can recognize similar dynamics in contemporary issues, such as systemic inequality, abuse of power, and the ongoing struggle for rights and recognition by marginalized groups. Thus, we can better understand the past and equip ourselves to address and challenge these injustices in the present.

Tamar's Other Brother

Tamar's ordeal continued beyond the initial violence inflicted upon her by her brother Amnon. After the assault, her other brother, Absalom, offered her refuge under his roof. However, this sanctuary came with a devastating condition: she was to remain silent about her trauma. Absalom's demand for her silence represented another layer of oppression, effectively denying Tamar the psychological safety and validation she needed to process her experience. By silencing her, Absalom perpetuated her suffering, forcing her to internalize her pain and degradation. Absalom's subsequent act of vengeance, murdering Amnon, was an attempt to address the wrong done to Tamar. Yet, this act of retribution failed to acknowledge or heal the enduring impact of the trauma that she endured. Tamar's story illustrates the complex dynamics of familial and societal responses to sexual violence, where physical protection is often offered at the expense of emotional and psychological healing. This scenario underscores the necessity of comprehensive support systems that validate and address the full spectrum of trauma survivors' experiences, ensuring their voices are heard and their healing prioritized.

Tamar's Legacy and Our Charge

The narrative of Tamar, laden with pain and resilience, serves as a clarion call to action. It compels us to confront the unsettling truths of our collective past and to advocate for a future free of such injustices. Tamar's legacy should inspire us to become lighthouses of hope, resilience, and transformation, dedicated to advancing justice and healing in our communities. Churches, in particular, must remain steadfast in our pursuit of truth and justice, compassionate in our interactions, and unwavering in our love for all humanity.

Amnon's and their cousin's betrayal of trust and the trauma inflicted upon Tamar illuminate the wounds still very present in today's world. This case underscores the complex emotions of betrayal, anger, and despair that often accompany such traumatic events. It further underscores the reality that both rape victim and rapist show up in our worship spaces.

Stories of sexual molestation by family members abound in our society. The victims are often silenced by fear, threats, and shame.

Chapter 56

Beginning in Judges 19: The Levite Who
Butchered His Concubine

IN JUDGES 19 IS a chilling, disturbing, and morally troubling account of misogyny, rape, human trafficking, murder, and dismemberment, where a Levite cuts up his concubine's body into twelve pieces. This act of violence has far-reaching theological ramifications that raise significant questions about the nature of humanity, deeply ingrained societal norms, how they can lead to collective trauma, and the role of faith in addressing systemic injustice.

As a collective faith community, we cannot exempt ourselves from the disquieting narrative of the Levite's concubine, or we will inadvertently perpetuate the silence surrounding the horrible experiences of those ensnared by human trafficking networks.

Concubines were women used for a man's pleasure (usually sexual pleasure) without the legal status of a primary wife. It is likely that she did not choose this status for herself. Right away, one sees that there is a power dynamic here. There's no mention of a wife, which I find ironic. The story goes that the concubine leaves the Levite and returns to her father's house in Bethlehem, possibly due to adultery or mistreatment. The Hebrew text uses the word *zanah*, usually translated as "prostitute" or "fornicate," to describe her actions. However, the Greek Septuagint version uses *orgizō*, meaning "to be angry," suggesting she left out of anger or discontent.[1] Why was she angry? Perhaps she was not the one to sit by while she is mistreated. The reason for the difference is unclear, but some interpret "prostitution" metaphorically, akin to how Jeremiah and Hosea use it to symbolize Israel and Judah's unfaithfulness to God. It appears the woman's departure was an act of autonomy, although the story reveals she had little autonomy herself. It's also important to pay attention to the different societies in which the interpretation and word use takes place: The Hebrew society may present as less liberal or open than the Greek society—just another thing to hold in tension.

So, according to the text, the Levite went after her, with gifts and a male attendant to speak to her heart, or in other words, to sweet talk her. If she did cheat, and he is there with gifts, then this is where the parallel to the Hosea passage would show up. Another side of that is if it is a case where he was physically or otherwise abusing her, and she left in anger and the Levite went after her, it would be a classic case of abuser's guilt. He feels guilty and now he is trying to win her back with gifts and the promise of a bright tomorrow. Of course, the abusing usually continues until, sadly, somebody may get killed.

The next thing we see is this four-day long negotiation between the Levite and the concubine's father. We don't know where she is during the festivities, but we haven't heard about her for these days. There's also no mention of her having any input in the negotiations. This is problematic. Night approached as they journeyed, and the servant suggested they stop in Jebus (later Jerusalem), a non-Israelite town. However, the Levite preferred to continue into Benjaminite territory, trusting "brothers" over "strangers."

---

1. See Krisel, "Was the Levite's Concubine."

Chapter 57

THEY EVENTUALLY REACHED GIBEAH, a town in Benjamin. Despite receiving no local hospitality, an Ephraimite living in Gibeah offered them shelter for the night. Judges 19:14–26 is straight out of *Disturbia*. For while in the home of the Ephraimite, some men from Gibeah came and demanded sexual favors from the Levite. The host tries to prevent what he terms as an evil thing from happening—perhaps not because of the same-gender sex, but because of how it would look for him. Now, in another shocking turn, the Ephraimite offered his virgin daughter and the Levite's concubine for their pleasure to avoid abusing a male visitor. This male visitor must be protected at all costs. This is all kinds of disgusting and problematic! The host offering his own daughter for what he may assume is to fulfill a sexual desire is evil.

In addition to that, he offers another woman with whom he has no (reported) connection. And the Levite, who just spoke tenderly to her, did not offer to defend her. This may cause one to think that the Greek word usage is closer to the truth—that she left him out of anger at his treatment of her. Further, how did the daughter and concubine feel about this offering? They are not given a voice.

After enduring a night of sexual abuse and dehumanization at the hands of the men at the door, the woman managed to reach the house where the next morning the Levite found her passed out. Upon seeing her, he instructs her to get up so they could leave. The way the story is told is that he opens the door and sees her there. Did he open the door to go looking for her? The text doesn't say. It is doubtful that he did, because there is no evidence in the text that he shows any concern at all for her well-being. His callous, "Get up, we are going" says much about his character. At his bidding, her violation has saved him from being violated. This is blood-curdling enough, and yet, it gets worse. Unable to awaken her, he placed her on a donkey and began the journey home.

Upon his return home, the Levite dismembered the concubine's body. There are four movements here used to describe what he did to her: took, seized, cut, and sent. The Hebrew text leaves ambiguity about whether she was already dead when he dismembered her, although the Levite later claims that she was. He claimed that his purpose in cutting her into twelve pieces was to expose the Gibeahites' sin to his tribal relations.

Chapter 58

IN JUDGES 20, THE Levite meets with representatives of the recipients of the body parts to explain. The Israelites gather at Mizpah, asking how this evil had occurred. The Levite's response emphasizes his innocence and portrays himself as the victim of the Gibeahites' intent to kill him, while leaving out key events from the earlier narrative. Notably, he omits that the men of Gibeah initially sought to have sex with him and resorted to taking the concubine as a last option. Moreover, he fails to mention that he actually sent the concubine out to the men of Gibeah, choosing her dehumanization over risking any harm to himself.

To add insult to injury, the Levite introduces certain alterations to the original narrative. He refers to the men of Gibeah as "lords" or "leaders" (Hebrew: *ba'ale*), potentially framing the attack as an official act of the city rather than the work of few, as previously implied. He also claims that the men "planned to kill" him, diverging from the suggestion that they sought sexual relations. Additionally, he states in his report that his concubine "died" due to the attack. There are all sorts of things wrong with this.

O what a tangled web. Now, because the tribe of Benjamin won't give up the guilty, a civil war erupted, resulting in the near-annihilation of the men of Benjamin in subsequent battles. This is terrible. But wait! There's more! The Israelites, remorseful for the loss of an entire tribe, looked to repopulate Benjamin. Their solution was to conquer the town of Jabesh-Gilead, slaughtering everyone except four hundred young virgins, whom they took as booty loot to repopulate Benjamin. Since there were not enough virgins from Jabesh-Gilead to accommodate all the men, virgins participating in a ritual celebration at Shiloh were abducted and given to the men of Benjamin. Thus, the punishment for rape was more rape.

Chapter 59

Exploring Themes in the Narrative

1. *Human Depravity and Violence*: What drives humans to commit such heinous acts? How do we talk about such acts and how do societies respond to such behavior?

2. *The Levite's Moral Responsibility*: The Levite's decision to cut up his concubine's body is a disturbing response to the abuse and violence she endured during her final moments. Theological discussions can revolve around the Levite's moral responsibility and whether his actions were justified or morally defensible in any way.

3. *Societal Norms and Patriarchy*: This account also sheds light on the prevailing societal norms and patriarchal structures of the time. It highlights how women, particularly those in vulnerable positions like concubines, were often subjected to violence and abuse without any recourse to justice. This raises further questions about the Bible's stance on gender equality and the treatment of women in ancient Israelite society.

4. *The Role of Faith and Religion*: The role of faith and religion here is complex. The Levite's profession as a religious figure adds another layer of difficulty to the story. Theological discussions can center on whether faith should be a force for justice and compassion or, as seen in this case, potentially used

to justify or perpetuate harm. What was the author's agenda in including this horror story?

5. *Systemic Injustice and Collective Trauma*: Judges 19 is a harrowing example of systemic injustice. The concubine's brutal treatment and the lack of accountability for her abusers mirror the systemic issues prevalent in society. Theological conversations can explore how these systemic injustices contribute to collective trauma and what faith communities can do to address and rectify such deep-seated problems (not remain silent).

6. *Reckoning with Difficult Texts*: Judges 19 presents a significant challenge to readers and theologians alike. It forces us to reckon with the more troubling aspects of biblical stories and the moral dilemmas they pose. How do we approach and interpret such texts in a way that promotes ethical reflection and growth?

7. *Redemptive Narratives*: Some theologians may look for redemptive elements here or in subsequent biblical texts. They may seek to identify moments of transformation or justice that counterbalance the horror of Judg 19. Exploring how biblical narratives evolve and respond to issues of injustice can be a valuable aspect of theological reflection. If there is no utility for resolution, the theologian should not force one.

8. *Lessons for Contemporary Society*: Finally, the story of the Levite and his concubine can be used as a lens through which to view contemporary issues of gender-based violence, systemic injustice, and the role of faith in promoting social justice. Theological discussions can explore how lessons from this narrative can inform modern approaches to addressing similar societal challenges.

Chapter 60

The Depths of Rage

GRIEF IS WHAT HAPPENS as a result of trauma. Grieving is what we do when grief is present. Sometimes, rage can emerge as a legitimate emotional response to the grief that we feel. To be clear, rage is not synonymous with violence but can serve as a catalyst for change. I mean, unless we feel some rage about some acts of injustice, no action will be taken to bring about change. Jesus' rage at the injustices around him were part of what motivated the tone of his ministry. What is crucial is how that rage is processed, understood, and ultimately, how it informs action. Like the psalmists, Christ-followers today can bring their full emotional selves into their faith communities and into their relationship with God. This includes their rage, which can be laid bare before a God who listens, understands, and calls us into paths of righteousness and justice.

The (Transformative) Power of Rage

Rage can mobilize individuals and communities to confront injustice, demand accountability, and work toward a more just society. When appropriately channeled, rage becomes a force for positive change, driving activism, advocacy, and community organizing.

Coping with rage in a healthy manner is also paramount. I use the term "healthy" here as a reminder that we begin with "First, do no harm." This involves creating safe spaces for dialogue, seeking therapy or counseling, and engaging in self-care practices. It's vital to recognize that rage can be a valid and transformative emotion, one that can guide us toward a more just and compassionate world.

The trauma of injustice, whether personal or systemic, is a complex and deeply affecting issue that reverberates through individuals and communities. By examining these biblical narratives, understanding the distinctions between personal and systemic injustice, and acknowledging the role of rage as a catalyst for change, we equip ourselves to respond more empathetically and effectively to the wounds inflicted by injustice.

Chapter 61

There is no death, daughter. People die only when we forget them. If you can remember me, I will be with you always.
—Isabel Allende, *Eva Luna*

David and Bathsheba in 2 Samuel

ALRIGHT, THE BOOK OF Samuel is not a standalone book. It is part of the narrative of Israel's monarchy. Second Samuel is part of a larger corpus of material that has a shared theological outlook. First and Second Samuel were originally one book and not two. The authorship is unknown, and both 1 and 2 Samuel are written from a later point of view after the monarchy ended, and likely during or even after the Babylonian exile itself. What we see here basically is a defending or spinning of David's legacy.

The Gaze and Conquest Mentality

The concept of the "gaze" is deeply rooted in gender, power, and cultural theory. The one who gazes is often in a position of power, rendering the object of the gaze vulnerable. David's gaze from his palace on Bathsheba is layered with meanings that extend beyond the mere act of looking. His position on the roof of the palace is no coincidence; it's a vantage point that affords him a panoramic view, emblematic of his territorial and societal control. He surveys his dominion both in terms of land and subjects, amplifying the problematic nature of his gaze.

The text here juxtaposes David's idleness in the palace with his army's engagement in war, adding a critical dimension to his "conquest mentality." He's not merely a warrior expanding his territorial boundaries; he is also a voyeur who seeks to extend his dominion in more insidious ways. His gaze on Bathsheba is symbolic of invasion, and a silent but potent assertion of his entitlement. If she wasn't naked, he would have stripped her with his eyes.

David's absence from the battlefield is also worth interrogating. While it is true that kings didn't always accompany their armies, the text emphasizes his decision to stay behind. In doing so, it invites us to speculate whether David's battlefield is different but no less predatory—a battlefield of personal desires and exploitations. His decision not to be physically present where one might expect him to be—leading his troops in battle—serves to highlight where he is instead: exerting his power in a domestic sphere, which has implications for the types of conquests he's interested in.

Further, it's essential to consider how this "conquest mentality" intersects with the social and theological constructs of the time. In a society where the king was seen as God's anointed, the wielding of power was often given divine sanction. David's sense of entitlement might have been bolstered by this theological framework, adding layers of complexity to our understanding of abuse and violence in a faith context. David didn't just "see" Bathsheba. He was predatorial in his looking.

Victim-Blaming and the Arts

Artistic representations don't just serve as illustrations but as interpretations, encoding complex ideas and cultural attitudes. When examining the depictions of Bathsheba, one must also pay attention to how these renderings are inherently an exercise in hermeneutics. The manner in which Bathsheba is portrayed in many artworks—seductive, inviting—does more than illustrate a scene; it shapes interpretation, often in ways that are dismissive of the woman's lived reality and trauma.

Artistic portrayals that depict Bathsheba as seductive participate in a larger, systemic cultural narrative that shifts the blame for sexual violence away from perpetrators and onto victims. This transference is certainly not neutral either, because it is an act of power. By framing Bathsheba as seductive, these artworks perpetuate a harmful myth, affecting not only the interpretation of the biblical text but also broader understandings of sexual violence.

Historically, when victims of sexual assault have reported their trauma, they have been questioned in ways that suggest that they somehow invited the assault. "What were you wearing?" "Why were you there?" "Why didn't you go with someone instead of going by yourself?" These reinforce a toxic narrative that, somehow, the victim is responsible for the crime committed against them. It is a damning and damaging perspective that has infiltrated even the retelling of biblical stories. The depictions of Bathsheba (and women) distort the truth. The power imbalance is obvious—he was the king, and Bathsheba had no real agency in the situation. Countless survivors, like Bathsheba, deserve to have their stories told without blame or suspicion.

Another clergywoman with whom I had a conversation about David and Bathsheba told me that "Bathsheba should have known better because she was a married woman." This is, sadly, the general consensus of too many people, including people in positions of authority and influence as a clergyperson. I was left to wonder, what has happened to congregants and the community at large when they have thought they could entrust the report of their abuse to this clergyperson only to discover that "there is no hiding place down here"?

Far too many cases of stepfathers and other family members assaulting children in the home have gone without recourse due to the "no confidence vote" by the adults to whom they made the reports. Stories abound where mothers have excommunicated their children to protect a man whom their children have accused of molesting them. The children are labeled as "fast," "troublesome," "rude," "liars," and even "jealous," leaving them even more vulnerable and a target for further trauma.

A few years ago, as the Florida Conference of The UMC sought to stand in solidarity with victims of sexual abuse, members of the conference wore buttons and badges with the words "I believe you." This essentially sent a message that we commit to listen without judgment and come alongside victims of sexual assault toward a pathway of healing. If only Bathsheba had such a community to go to and rely on!

Chapter 62

THE TEXT OF 2 SAM 11 itself offers no support for the notion that Bathsheba was an active, willing participant in the events that unfolded. In fact, the textual evidence suggests that Bathsheba's agency is stripped away from her at multiple levels. For example, she is introduced only through her relationships with men—she is "the wife of Uriah the Hittite" and the "daughter of Eliam." Such introductions serve to objectify her, situating her as a mere extension of the men in her life rather than as someone with her own autonomy and agency. By introducing her in this way, the text unwittingly participates in the diminution of her humanity, as if she was no more than an object in David's—and by extension, society's—conquest mentality.

Moreover, Bathsheba's actions in the narrative are described almost entirely in the passive voice. She "was sent for," "came," and "returned to her house." The text situates her as an object moved by forces external to her, underscoring her lack of agency in this traumatic event. There's no mutual affection or consent mentioned; Bathsheba is summoned, taken, and then dismissed. This motif shows up again in the rape of Tamar.

Thus, to portray Bathsheba as in any way seductive is not just to misread the text; it is to participate in a harmful interpretive tradition that has very real, damaging implications for how society understands and engages with victims of sexual violence. The Bible and the arts that it has inspired must both be scrutinized for the ways in which they may perpetuate harmful power dynamics and gendered assumptions. By doing so, one takes a necessary step toward a more honest and ethically responsible engagement with sacred texts and their ongoing interpretation in culture and scholarship.

Chapter 63

A Calculated Inquiry

THE PHRASEOLOGY OF DAVID's "inquiry" into Bathsheba's identity is significant in the Hebrew text. The term used, *darash*, embodies multiple nuances including seeking, inquiring, and investigating.[1] The multivalence of this term captures the essence of David's actions—predatory, calculated, and intentional. This was a targeted search and a reconnaissance to acquire critical information that would serve his desires.

It did not appear to bother him that Bathsheba was married. Rather, it seemed to further stimulate his illicit intentions. One must ask why the knowledge of her marital status did not deter him. The text implies that David's power and sense of entitlement, amplified by his position as the anointed king, rendered such ethical and social norms as marriage irrelevant. Here, the reality of David's authority meets the raw vulnerability of Bathsheba's social position. This interaction presents a critical moment of character revelation: David is not just a man of passion but a man of calculation. He assesses the situation and proceeds despite the ethical and moral costs.

If we consider the possibility that Bathsheba might have been in her mid-teens, the ethical gravity of this episode intensifies considerably. The age dynamic would introduce an imbalance of

---

1. Strong, *New Strong's Exhaustive Concordance*, #1875.

social or marital power and one of physical and psychological development. A teenage Bathsheba would likely have far less agency and ability to assert herself than an older woman. Even if the text doesn't explicitly state her age, historical context allows for such a reading, and it introduces another layer of exploitation to this already complex power dynamic. Her youth would make her even more vulnerable to the whims of a powerful older man, accentuating the egregiously exploitative nature of David's actions.

Considering Bathsheba's probable young age, David's inquiry moves beyond the boundaries of simple unethical behavior to a domain of deeply entrenched abuse and exploitation. It questions both the nature of David's kingship and the cultural and theological constructs that could enable such an abuse of power.

Hence, the inquiry serves as a narrative lens through which we can dissect multiple layers of abuse: it is patriarchal, in that it ignores Bathsheba's agency and personhood as a woman; it is ethically blind, as it disregards her marital status; and it is potentially age-exploitative. Together, these layers compile into a disturbing portrait of David, forcing us to grapple with how power and entitlement manifest within sacred narratives and what ethical responsibilities we hold in interpreting and teaching these texts.

R. Kelly, Harvey Weinstein, Donald Trump, Sean Combs, Clarence Thomas, leaders in the church and far too many other men of influence who have been accused and sometimes convicted of sexual misconduct, still have "protectors" in society. Society has often been more concerned about "protecting" these predators than about holding them accountable, transforming the processes that allow them to abuse their power and get away with it, and helping the victims to heal. The laws that force a woman to carry a pregnancy by rape to term is an example of how the female body has been often co-opted and discarded as a disposable product.

Chapter 64

Power Dynamics and Lack of Agency

THE WAY BATHSHEBA IS introduced in the text is widely suggestive that she exists within the context of her father and her husband. Here, she is already in a diminished capacity. In the narrative of 2 Sam 11:4–5, the language is markedly devoid of mutuality. David "sends for her" and "takes her," with the verbs unambiguously marking Bathsheba as the object of his actions. There is no dialogue recorded between David and Bathsheba, no opportunity provided for her to express either consent or refusal. She is an object, acquired and acted upon. Bathsheba, within this structure, possesses virtually no agency; she is wholly subject to David's authority and desires. Her agency is further marginalized by the fact that she is impregnated, a condition that inevitably would limit her social and economic choices within her cultural context even further.

This record of David's actions finds a potent and unsettling precursor in 1 Sam 8:11–18, where the prophet Samuel provides a divinely inspired warning about the dangers of kingship. Here, the people are cautioned that a king will "take" their sons, daughters, fields, and vineyards. The Hebrew verb *laqach*, translated as "take," forms a disturbing linguistic and thematic bridge between the warning in 1 Sam 8 and the narrative in 2 Sam 11.[1] David has

---

1. Brown et al., *Hebrew and English Lexicon*, 542.

become precisely the type of king Samuel warned against—a taker, an exploiter of his people's resources and, in Bathsheba's case, of their very bodies and lives.

What's more is that the term *mishpatim*, which appears in 1 Sam 8:11, adds another layer to this complex tableau. Generally translated as "judgments" or "justice," here it characterizes the king's actions, revealing an unnerving distortion of justice. If *mishpatim*—ordinarily associated with equity, fairness, and divine right—can be manipulated to include a king's prerogative to take whatever he wishes without consent or repercussion, what does this say about the architecture of power and authority in Israel? And by extension, what does it challenge in our theological and ethical frameworks today?

What we encounter here is a form of "justice" that is not only human but egregiously patriarchal and monarchical. The justice of God, meant to be restorative and equitable, is subverted into a justice that protects and further entrenches David's power at the expense of Bathsheba's agency. This narrative moment in 2 Sam 11 then serves not only as a denouncement of David but also as an indictment of a system that enables such a distortion of divine justice.

This story offers an unsettling view into how power is exercised, abused, and legitimized within the structures of ancient Israel, and by extension, how such systems continue to echo in our contemporary settings. For those of us who engage with these texts, the narrative compels us to interrogate the actions of individuals and the systems that authorize such actions. It serves as a sobering reminder of how far-removed human institutions—be they monarchies or even religious communities—can become from God's intention for justice and right relationship.

Chapter 65

The Anointed King and His Power

THE CHRONICLE OF DAVID'S rise to power encapsulates a tension intrinsic to the Hebrew Scriptures and, indeed, to religious thought more broadly: the confluence of divine anointing with earthly authority. David, anointed by the prophet Samuel in 1 Sam 16, does not fully come into his monarchical role until 2 Sam 5. Yet even before he sits on the throne, the epithet of being "God's anointed" trails him, offering a religious sanctification to his subsequent actions and decisions. By the time he consolidates power, establishing his capital and defeating his enemies, his authority seems irrefutable, underscored not just by military might but by a presumed divine endorsement.

This blending of divine anointing and earthly power is troubling. It conflates power with purity. David is not simply a king; he is God's anointed king. Therefore, his actions—be they acts of war, governance, or as is the case in 2 Sam 11, personal conduct—become dangerously susceptible to being perceived as above reproach. The very title of "God's anointed" can convert actions that should be subject to moral and ethical scrutiny into acts that are instead sanctified by the cloak of religiosity.

This equation of divine anointing with moral purity or ethical rightness has serious ramifications, especially when examining incidents of sexual violence like that perpetrated against Bathsheba.

When an individual's authority is seen as divinely endorsed, their actions, however questionable, can readily be excused or rationalized as having a divine sanction. It also creates a space where the voice of the marginalized is stifled, their suffering deemed inconsequential, and their humanity minimized, all in the name of adhering to a supposed divine ordaining of power dynamics. This is currently unfolding in the US with the cult-like following of Donald Trump by evangelicals, et al.

We are faced with these challenges of reconsidering how religious institutions and religious language can sometimes sanctify systemic inequalities and abuses of power. In the structures of many faith communities, leadership is often believed to be ordained by God, and thus, the actions of those leaders are granted an implicit theological weight. While the belief in divinely ordained leadership is not problematic in and of itself, it becomes deeply troubling when used to legitimize actions that are contrary to the principles of justice, equity, and compassion that are foundational to decency. This is not only about David's actions but also of the systems and beliefs that enabled him. It becomes a prophetic call to disentangle the intricate web of power and divine anointing.

The Cover-Up and Its Aftermath

The tragic unfolding of events post-David's sexual violation of Bathsheba culminates in a bleak irony: the death of their son. David's failed cover-up and the orchestrated murder of Bathsheba's husband, Uriah, highlight the systemic failure to recognize her suffering. While the text sees the child's death as divine retribution against David, it offers no redress to Bathsheba's own traumatic experiences. The text remains silent on her suffering, focusing instead on David's moral and spiritual failings and his subsequent response.

Bathsheba endures multiple traumas—sexual violence, widowhood, and the death of her child—yet her story is subsumed under David's sin and repentance.

PART 2: BIBLE TALK

The omission of Bathsheba's experience in the text forces us to think about how we create space for survivors in our own religious contexts.

Chapter 66

The Cover-Up and Its Aftermath Within a Larger System
—2 Samuel 12:15–19

THE EVENTS FOLLOWING THE sexual violence inflicted upon Bathsheba are both harrowing and indicative of the systemic failure to acknowledge her trauma. The aftermath begins with David's elaborate scheme to cover up his violation, an attempt to preserve his reputation that further silences Bathsheba and reduces her to a mere pawn in the unfolding drama. When the initial cover-up fails, David resorts to arranging the death of Uriah, Bathsheba's husband. This sequence of decisions signifies a continued trajectory of violence that implicates not only David but also the network of power and authority that supports him.

Bathsheba, now a widow and a bereaved mother, remains a silenced figure in this unfolding drama, with the text granting her scarcely any space to articulate her anguish, loss, or trauma. The child's death is interpreted by the narrator as a divine act of retribution against David, but this interpretation offers no comfort or justice to Bathsheba. The death of the child does not act as a corrective to the abuse she endured but serves as another marker of her objectification and marginalization. Even her loss is co-opted into a theological framework that centers David's sin and divine punishment, further sidelining her experience and suffering. While the text does not explicitly get into Bathsheba's psyche, it is impossible to overlook the fact that she is not given any space in the text to grieve. And when David was prompted to repent, he did not mention her.

This omission represents a form of epistemic violence, a silencing of voices and stories that should be integral to the narrative. This is particularly consequential because it mirrors a persistent problem in both religious and societal discussions surrounding sexual violence: the prioritization of the powerful perpetrator's narrative over that of the victim. Whether by focusing on the perpetrator's reputation, potential for redemption, or the supposed divine ramifications of their actions, these frameworks often neglect the lived experiences and sustained traumas of the survivors.

Bathsheba's virtual silence in the text challenges us to reconsider the narrative spaces and platforms we offer to survivors of sexual violence within our own religious and theological contexts. It invites us to ask who gets to articulate their experience of God in the aftermath of trauma, who gets to interpret suffering, and who remains silenced in the interpretive traditions of our faith communities. The erasure of Bathsheba's voice from this theological narrative should serve as a stark reminder of the work that remains to be done in amplifying marginalized voices, particularly in conversations surrounding power, violence, and divine justice.

Chapter 67

Another Side of King David

DAVID SHOWED UP IN this narrative as a thug who hired himself out as a hit man and who had his own band of hitmen. He cheated Uriah out of his life and his wife and any children they might have had together in their future. True to his nature, David had the nerve to pray to God: *Against thee only have I sinned.* Against God and only God. He did not even mention Bathsheba. The editor of the Psalms had to add her name to explain what he was talking about.

Despite the great press that David gets, and even though the text is quite ambiguous with its language, this David-Bathsheba saga can be judged as rape, given the power dynamics at work. There is nothing to overtly suggest that David forced her. However, it's not enough to conclude that the sexual encounter between the two was consensual simply because the text doesn't explicitly state otherwise. One must read behind, in front, and within the text in order to get a fuller picture. Think of David's style, position, life, privilege, etc., in light of Bathsheba's. Take into consideration the absolute power of an ancient Near Eastern monarch combined with the absence of her husband to protect her, and one may see how that significantly reduces Bathsheba's ability to consent to the sexual encounter. She may not have been hit over the head with a club and dragged by the hair to David's cave, but she is nonetheless a captive because to come to the king when called is not necessarily to consent.

Notes on Reading Bathsheba's Story

Consider these lenses when reading Bathsheba's story:

1. *Centering Bathsheba's Perspective*: We can prioritize Bathsheba's experience and agency within the narrative. It could explore her role, feelings, and choices in the context of her relationship with David, emphasizing her voice and her story.

2. *Power and Vulnerability*: Another approach may highlight the power dynamics at play in Bathsheba's encounter with King David. It could examine how Bathsheba's position as a woman and a wife of a hitman may have made her vulnerable to David's advances.

3. *Intersectionality*: Womanist theology often considers intersectionality, acknowledging how factors like gender, race, and social status intersect to shape individuals' experiences. In the case of Bathsheba, both her identity as a woman and her status in relation to whom she is married may be explored.

4. *Ethical Reflection*: We may engage in ethical reflection on issues such as consent, accountability, and justice within the narrative. We could challenge traditional readings and encourage readers to grapple with the moral complexities of the story.

5. *Empowerment and Healing*: A womanist perspective may emphasize Bathsheba's resilience and potential for empowerment. It could explore how Bathsheba's role as the mother of Solomon signifies her influence and agency in shaping the future of Israel's monarchy.

6. *Redemption and Transformation*: Similar to traditional interpretations, a redemptive-type reading might consider the potential for redemption and transformation in the narrative,

particularly in David's response to the prophet Nathan's rebuke and his acknowledgment of wrongdoing.

Chapter 68

"My heart is possessed by pain. There is a searing unlike any other and one which I cannot describe except in tears and the outbursts that have taken hold of my heart. On August 24th, one week before my son's 24th birthday, the police came to my home to inform me that my son died at the scene of an accident he was involved in. I cannot shake the unbearable pain that I feel. I keep going back in my mind and seeing the police at the door, hearing the conversation, and feeling the searing that won't let up. I am confused. This does not make any sense. There is nothing in this life that supports this madness.

"My son's name is Arleigh Hartfield Byer II. He is my second-born. I love him fiercely, as I do my children. I miss him deeply. He was not supposed to die at age 23. I am a mother whose grief cannot be comforted. I am inconsolable. The path that I have walked with others is completely unfamiliar to me. It is not the same path. My grief knows no bounds." (Journal excerpt)

TEARS AT THE ALTAR, LAMENT IN MY BREASTS

Psalm 88—O the Shame

Background and Historical Context

THERE ARE MULTIPLE WITNESSES to the reality of pain and multiple shapes of containers in the canon. Psalm 88 is said to be an "embarrassment to conventional faith" and is one of the eleven in the Korahite collection. It is penned by Heman the Ezrahite, who we are introduced to as a wise figure in 1 Kgs 4:31. The psalm likely emerged from a post-exilic context where the community wrestled with existential questions of God's character, justice, and the ongoing experience of suffering. However, it is so timeless that it transcends any single historical moment, providing a framework for us to address God in the midst of despair.

Literary Structure

The psalm exhibits a carefully constructed literary structure, replete with the use of parallelisms, metaphorical language, and rhetorical questions. (It also lacks a developed petition.) You will not find this psalm in the lectionary. It is not a pretty psalm that follows the usual pattern of invocation, complaint, petition, expression of trust, and vow of praise.

In addition to the superscription, verses 2–3 contain the invocation and initial pleas, while verses 4–10a form the first complaint consisting of a description of suffering and an accusation. Verses 10b–13 constitute the second complaint and can be subdivided into a description of prayer and a contestation of God. The third complaint can be found in verses 14–19 and can be divided into three parts: a description of prayer, an accusation of God, and a description of suffering.

Some observations: the introductory laments all have the name of YHWH; they all contain variations of lament verbs: call, calling, cry, crying, call for help; and they portray a climactic time frame: by day, in the night, every day, in the morning. In my culture, we simply say, "Morning, noon, and night."

In the middle section of the psalm, we find mention of God's justice, care, faithfulness, etc., surrounded by nothing but bleakness—hurt, accusations, loneliness, a sense of abandonment, etc. Now, all of this is being poured out from the heart and mouth of a worship leader. Can you imagine what this song sounds like? It makes, "Hello darkness, my old friend," seem like "Jesus loves me this I know." It is harrowing.

Parallelism

Hebrew poetry is known for its employment of parallelism, where lines or sets of lines mirror or contrast with each other in structure, meaning, or both. Psalm 88 employs synonymous and antithetical parallelisms, adding depth and emphasis to the expressions of lament. For example, the lines "I am overwhelmed with troubles and my life draws near to death" (v. 3 NIV) employ synonymous parallelism, reinforcing the psalmist's condition of utter despair. The repetition serves to underline the severity and all-encompassing nature of the psalmist's suffering.

Metaphorical Language

The psalm also incorporates tons of metaphorical language to communicate its themes. Phrases like "the depths" (v. 6) or being "among the dead" (v. 5) help us understand the psalmist's state of deep despair. Such language provides an artistic avenue for expressing what could otherwise be indescribable experiences of human suffering.

Rhetorical Questions

The psalm further deploys rhetorical questions, such as "Do you show your wonders to the dead?" (v. 10 NIV), to build an argument and to challenge conventional notions of God's deliverance. These questions serve to heighten the tension between the presumed character of God and the experience of the psalmist, thereby inviting the reader into a reflective theological space. Perhaps they are also asked in an effort to move God to action as a God of salvation. So far, we have not seen anything that can be clearly defined as God's salvation in this psalm.

Themes and Theological Considerations

1. *Suffering and Marginality*: In its relentless focus on the experience of suffering, Ps 88 does more than offer an outlet for individual lament; it also gives voice to collective experiences of marginality. The psalmist's despair can be seen as a microcosm of the suffering experienced by those on the margins of society—whether due to systemic injustice, racial inequality, or economic disparity. Additionally, the focus on suffering and marginality in Ps 88 encourages a rethinking of traditional theodicies. It raises the question: How do we talk about God's goodness and justice when confronted with the ubiquitous realities of suffering, especially the suffering of the marginalized? It pushes us to eschew simplistic answers and instead engage deeply with the complexities inherent in the intersection of theology, ethics, and social justice.

2. *Role of Community*: The pronounced absence of a communal voice in Ps 88 distinguishes it from other psalms where the lament or praise is collective. This solipsistic focus on individual suffering draws attention to the interplay between personal and communal laments. How does individual suffering relate to collective suffering? Can one be fully understood apart from the other? What does the absence of community in this psalm say about the limits and possibilities of communal liturgical practices?

Furthermore, the individuality of the lament in Ps 88 challenges us to examine how community can be a space that either amplifies the voices of suffering or silences them. This leads into a broader theological exploration about the ecclesiological dimensions of lament.

3. *Absence of Resolution*: What sets Ps 88 apart most distinctly is its absence of a vow of praise or narrative resolution. Most lament psalms conclude with a turning point, a moment where the psalmist reaffirms trust in God despite the preceding complaints. This psalm defies that structure. The absence of such resolution in Ps 88 makes it an anomaly, demanding exegetical attention to understand its place within the Psalter and its implications for theology. It serves as an ideological counterpoint to the concept of a perpetually responsive, omnipresent God, urging us to wrestle with the complexities of divine absence.

This deviation invites questions about the intent and impact of such a structure. Could the lack of resolution be a form of resistance, a refusal to submit to theological platitudes? Does it invite the reader, and more broadly the faith community, to sit with the tension between the experience of suffering and the absence of divine intervention? Does it challenge the inclination to conclude narratives of suffering with simplistic solutions, thus encouraging a more nuanced and inclusive theology? How do we articulate a theology that acknowledges both the attributes of God's compassion and the harsh realities of divine silence? The "unfinished" nature of this psalm can be seen as a deliberate attempt to preserve that tension, compelling us to live with and reflect upon the complexities rather than rush to premature conclusions. It truly complicates simplistic theodicies and invites us to consider how to speak of God's goodness in contexts that don't easily resolve into narratives of hope and triumph.

4. *Interrogating Theodicy*: This invites critical scrutiny into how we talk about God's goodness in contexts of unrelenting suffering and despair. Can a theodicy that doesn't make room for the unresolved suffering depicted in Ps 88 be considered sufficiently robust or even honest? Psalm 88 serves as an unflinching testament to the harsh realities of human existence,

challenging our theological paradigms and inviting us into dialogue with The More Than. It is a text that engages not just with personal lament but also with systemic issues, particularly when viewed through the lens of a theology that takes seriously the experiences and voices of those on the margins.

Chapter 69

Whose wife will she be?
—LUKE 20:33

Luke 20:27–38: They Ask of Resurrection

THEY SAY WHEN A person marries, they marry not only their spouse but the spouse's entire family. I understand the family connection, but literally marrying seven brothers? As this passage in Luke 20 is read through my womanist, grieving, advocacy lens, it presents multiple problems. It is likely that the Sadducees came to Jesus with a hypothetical and not an actual situation. Nevertheless, Levirate law itself is problematic.

The Problem of Levirate Marriage

The way the language is set up in the passage, the man acts in the active voice by "taking the woman in marriage." On the other hand, the woman acts in the passive voice by being given in marriage. The way Luke tells it, the woman had no choice in the matter. The Sadducees' question suggests here that the woman would or should continue to be a breeding tool in the event that there was a resurrection. The Gospel according to Mark also tells a version of this encounter. Warren Carter does not mince words in his comments that levirate marriage "ensures the woman's body and reproductive capacity serve male values, and provides no space for the woman's agency, choice, will or even well-being."[1]

The Questioners

The Sadducees were one of the elite religious sects of their day. Although they were often associated and sometimes mixed up with the Pharisees—another religious sect—there are stark differences between these two groups. For instance, though deeply religious, the Sadducees loved rubbing shoulders with the political puppets who were set up by Rome. You would never find them challenging the status quo, because if they did, it almost certainly would mean that they would lose some of their creature comforts that they seemingly cared about more than they did the lives of the people. Not only did they not challenge the status quo, they were very hard on anyone who did. One might imagine that with Jesus' work, which demonstrated an order that constantly challenged Rome, the Sadducees gritted their teeth each time they heard about the man from Galilee.[2] The Pharisees on the other hand, did not bother so much with the political structures of the day. They would accommodate any government in place as long as they were allowed to continue enjoying their positions of wheeling and dealing the religious life of the people in whatever ways they chose to. The danger of these two groups' attitudes should not be lost on us.

Another stark difference between these two powerful groups is where they draw or don't draw the religious boundaries. The Sadducees accepted only the books attributed to Moses, while the Pharisees accepted all the Scriptures with all the rules both oral and ceremonial. In addition to the difference in how they treat the Scriptures, the Pharisees believed in angels and the resurrection. In contrast, the Sadducees did not believe in any of that. There appeared to be a kind of rivalry between these two groups as well, and it is likely

---

1. Carter, *Mark*, 339.
2. Fallon, *Gospel According to St. Luke*, 300.

that the Sadducees' question to Jesus was designed to throw shade on the Pharisees and their belief in the resurrection.

Co-Opting the Woman's Womb

There seems to be an unhealthy fascination with the female body that can be traced all the way back to antiquity. Throughout the church's history, more policies are centered on defining and restricting the woman's body—what it wears, what it weighs, what is its complexion, what is its height, and a host of other nonsensically constructed articles.

If we put this Luke 20 passage in conversation with God's command to care for the widows, orphans, and strangers, there might be some stuttering happening. In an arrangement such as levirate marriage, the only way a widow has access to land and other means of support is if she is married to the brother of her dead childless husband. A woman would have worked and contributed to the family's wealth, yet she would have no say or ownership in the affairs of the household purse. It appears that instead of her inheriting property, she becomes part of the inheritance. She is seen merely as property.

Now let this passage with its patriarchal, misogynistic bias listen to Luke 1—Mary's album release prominently featuring her revolutionary Magnificat. Ooh now! Mary, of course, would have known of levirate marriage. And in her sassy rendition, the Sadducees with their pomposity and privilege would be found on the other side of God's kingdom.

Chapter 70

Preaching After the Death of My Son:
John 11:28–37

HAVE YOU SEEN ALL the ads on TV for medications? Pay attention to the side effects: "Stop using if you develop shortness of breath, swelling of the tongue, or blindness in your right eye. Do not use if you stop breathing." Seriously? These side effects are rattled off while the actors are smiling and having a grand time supposedly because they have used the medication advertised.

I have a hard time reconciling the image of the smiling tennis player with the long list of side effects. Yet, I also wonder about how closely this resembles life sometimes. We hear one thing, but we are seeing another thing. Someone might display a smile full of hope but the side effects say that, at any moment, things could fall apart. Even as a follower of Christ, this is true. Suffering, hurt, pain, and devastation can come even while the sun is shining. Life can be just like those medication ads.

I imagine that as Lazarus laid there drawing his last breaths, hopeful that Jesus would show up because, after all, they were good friends, and Jesus has done some really out of the box things before. Four days later, Mary and Martha shuffle dejectedly about their home, having lost their brother and maybe a little faith in their friend, Jesus. Have you ever been there? I think about how when Jesus came to visit, Martha spared no expense in time, talent, or treasure to lay out a spread for him because they were friends. I think about how Mary risked a possible stoning by remaining in the room and sitting at Jesus' feet, daring to talk to him, because they were friends. After all of that, when they needed Jesus, he did not show. Martha, who cooked up a storm and loved to set a spread, saw food and had no appetite. Mary, who defied the Godless laws of the day to sit at Jesus' feet, watched her strength ebb away. Have you ever been there?

I think of the question that the Jews asked at the end of the passage: "Could not he who opened the eyes of the blind man, stop this man from dying?" Could he have not stopped this dream from dying? Could he have not stopped this pain from breaking into this man's family? Lazarus is not supposed to die when you call Jesus "friend." Lazarus is not supposed to die when you do the best you can to be faithful to the tenets of Christianity. It is the classic "in a perfect world" scenario.

We have been falsely taught to go on as if we don't feel the pain. This harmful teaching has translated into the church where we rush to where Jesus raises Lazarus, having trampled over the verses before this event. Before we get to the raising, Lazarus dies, and Martha and Mary are grieving. This is happening in real time, and they do not know that Jesus will do the impossible. All they know is that their brother is dead and that mess hurts like hell. Have you been there? We rush to that place because we prefer to say that we are blessed and highly favored even when we don't feel like it's true. Or, because we have been scared into hiding from our own pain. That's why we often do not know what to do with people who are authentic in their grief. We may want to rush them outside because it makes us feel comfortable. We don't want to deal with their tears because we may not have dealt with ours. We judge them because we don't want to identify with them. And yet, the question is, Have you been there?

Somebody probably told Mary and Martha that their brother was "taken" to make them into better people. Someone probably told them that their brother was "taken" so that God could teach them some lessons to make them even more powerful in the community. Somebody must have told them that God "took" their brother because God takes the best. Suffering is not a glorious initiative. There is nothing romantic about losing someone you love. Suffering does not make anybody holier.

I'm going to make an intelligent guess that there has been at least one time in your life when like the sisters, you have declared, "Jesus, if you had been here . . ." I'm talking about that time, when hell broke loose and you cried, "Jesus, if you had been here . . ." Have you ever been there? Of course you have.

Jesus didn't stay away because he was uncomfortable with their pain. When Jesus finally shows up, he doesn't tell them, "O Mary don't you weep, don't you mourn." He does not tell Martha that she'll get over it. When he finally shows up, he does not remind them that they have cried enough. He does not tell them that God needed another flower, and that is why God picked their brother. You know why? Because it is all garbage and baseless.

Instead, Jesus asks: "Where have you laid him?" Let me put it this way: Where have you laid your burden? Where have you hidden your hurts? Where have you stashed away your disappointment? Where have you drowned your sorrows? "Come and see," they said. Come and see where my scars are. Come and see where my heartbreak is. Come and see where the accident occurred. Come see where I almost lost my mind.

Jesus' response: he weeps. Hmmm. That is a God I can deal with; not your god that is too thin-skinned to deal with my hurt and questions or backs away from me in my time of need or has no clue how to love me in my pain. I want this God who can cry, who sits with me in my sorrow, who shows up and cleans my bathroom, who cooks meals for my family, who does not judge or criticize that I am crying instead of talking. Yes, I want and need the God who loves. In seasons of distress and grief, love is a balm; love is salvation when your heart hurts so bad that it fails to function as it should.

Chapter 71

Crucifying Trauma

Why is it important to read the crucifixion through the lens of trauma?

GENERALLY, I DON'T WATCH what are called Bible movies. Based on the descriptions I heard, I would classify *The Passion of the Christ* as a horror movie—just because I am a lightweight. So, it took some convincing for me to watch it in the first place. Be that as it may, Mel Gibson did a fantastic job (in my opinion) of depicting the passion of Jesus. Though nobody is asking me, I will state further that he has done a far better job of doing a close reading of the passion narrative than has historically happened in our churches. He captured emotions and nuances and offered a long-awaited critique of how the story has been historically told. I didn't receive anything in exchange for saying that, and I have no desire to watch it again. I still believe it is a horror show.

Reading the passion story through the lens of trauma provides a richer, more nuanced understanding of the narrative. It bridges the gap between the divine and the human, allows for deeper empathy with those who suffer, challenges overly simplistic interpretations, and fosters a deeper appreciation of the Christian story of redemption.

The Importance of a Trauma-Informed Approach

Approaching the passion narrative through the lens of trauma is crucial for several reasons. Firstly, it grounds the narrative in the reality of human suffering. Christ's agony in the garden, his betrayal, his trials, the physical and emotional brutality of his crucifixion, and his sense of abandonment on the cross ("My God, my God, why have you forsaken me?") are not just theological motifs but real experiences of trauma.

Secondly, this perspective helps us relate more deeply to the human experience of Jesus, breaking down the notion of an impassive, distant deity, and instead presenting a God who truly partakes in the full spectrum of human experience, including pain, betrayal, and death. It underscores the Christian belief in a God who is "Emmanuel"—God with us, even in our most traumatic moments.

Contrasting Traditional Approaches

Traditionally, the passion narrative has often been approached with an emphasis on the triumph of resurrection, sometimes to the point of overshadowing the real suffering of Christ. The focus on the "willing sacrifice" of Jesus can inadvertently romanticize the cross, presenting it as a preordained event that glorifies suffering itself.

This perspective, while emphasizing the salvific nature of Christ's sacrifice, can sometimes neglect the true horror and injustice of the crucifixion. It can create an impression that suffering is inherently redemptive or that Jesus, in his divinity, was somehow above the human experience of trauma.

In particular, the Gospel of John presents a more composed picture of the crucifixion. It might be John's personality here. When we read the passion through the lens of trauma, the narrative shifts. Here, the focus is on the human experience of Jesus—his physical pain, emotional abandonment, and psychological distress. This perspective does not negate the redemptive aspect of the passion; instead, it adds depth to it.

This approach also challenges the notion that divinity is incompatible with or completely separate from the experience of trauma. If Jesus is fully divine and fully human, his divinity does not exempt him from human suffering. Instead, it deepens the incarnation's significance—God is not distant from human anguish but fully present in it.

Reading the passion through the lens of trauma also allows for a more insightful identification with those who suffer. It presents a Jesus who is not only a triumphant savior but also a fellow sufferer. This perspective can be particularly meaningful for individuals and communities who have experienced trauma, offering them a model of God who truly understands and shares in their pain. It respects the theological significance of Jesus' sacrifice. It also acknowledges the raw reality of suffering involved. This approach invites us to grapple with the complexities of the incarnation and the paradox of a God who is both all-powerful and vulnerable.

Chapter 72

Rethinking Redemption and Suffering

IF WE ASSERT THAT Christ's death is redemptive, it is essential to explore what we mean by redemption. Does finding redemption in Christ's suffering mean we find something inherently good in the suffering itself? A trauma-informed approach allows us to see redemption not as the glorification of suffering, but as God's ability to bring good out of a tragic and unjust event. It's about God's victory over suffering and death, rather than the suffering itself being good.

In this light, redemption is about resurrection and new life emerging from the depths of despair and death, rather than a divine endorsement of suffering. It invites believers to find God's presence not in causing suffering but in enduring and overcoming it.

Understanding the Cost of Redemption

Finally, viewing the passion through a trauma lens helps in comprehending the immense cost of redemption. It couples the sweet with the bitter entailed in the act of salvation, enriching the appreciation for the redemptive work accomplished through the crucifixion and resurrection of Christ.

The Political Temperature

The crucifixion of Jesus occurs at a time of heightened political tension. Roman occupation looms heavily over Judea, with the Jewish populace bearing the brunt of Roman authority and taxation. The presence of different Jewish groups, from the zealots advocating for rebellion to the Pharisees attempting to maintain religious purity, further complicates the political landscape. Into this milieu steps Jesus, whose teachings and actions, while primarily spiritual, inevitably make political statements—challenging the status quo and attracting the attention of both Jewish and Roman leaders. His entry into Jerusalem, hailed as a king, sets the stage for a political clash, inadvertently positioning him as a figure of subversion in the eyes of Roman authority.

A Series of Terrible Events

Betrayal of Friends

The narrative in Mark 14:43–50 paints a stark picture of betrayal. Judas, one of Jesus' closest followers, betrays him with a kiss—a symbol of friendship and trust turned into a signal for arrest. This act of betrayal by a confidant adds a layer of personal anguish to Jesus' ordeal. Similarly, Peter, who had sworn fidelity to Jesus, denies knowing him three times. This denial, fulfilling Jesus' own prediction, signifies Peter's human failing and underscores the overwhelming loneliness and misunderstanding Jesus faces, even among his closest followers.

Unjust Condemnation and Rigged Courts

Mark 14:53–65 describes a trial that is a travesty of justice. The religious authorities are determined to condemn Jesus, regardless of the evidence or lack thereof. False witnesses come forward, but their testimonies do not agree. Jesus, mostly silent, finally speaks to affirm his identity as the Messiah, which leads to accusations of blasphemy. The guy couldn't win for losing. Damned if he did, and damned if he did not. This scene exemplifies how legal and religious systems, meant to uphold truth and justice, can dovetail and become tools of oppression. We're right at home here, aren't we?

Isolation and Sense of Abandonment by God

Perhaps one of the most harrowing aspects of the crucifixion narrative is the deep sense of isolation and abandonment experienced by Jesus, depicted in Mark 15:34. Mocked, beaten, and crowned with thorns, Jesus is not only physically brutalized but also psychologically and spiritually isolated. His cry, "Eloi, Eloi, lema sabachthani?" ("My God, my God, why have you forsaken me?"), is an outright expression of desolation, indicating a moment of deep spiritual crisis. Could Jesus be having a crisis of faith?

Chapter 73

The Weeping of the Women

THESE ARE SOME OF the emotions that Jesus felt. It is disturbing than anyone would be put through that kind of torture. We feel the distress of this happening to our beloved Jesus. If we are honest, this is not a Jesus-alone historical event. This has happened to other human beings in various forms; drawing and quartering, being boiled in oil, and other evil ways. Another point to this is that the execution of Jesus did not happen only to Jesus. Many others were affected both by what they witnessed and by what they had hoped for.

Particularly, I am interested in the women who were at the crucifixion. The presence and reaction of the women, including Jesus' mother, in Mark 15:40–41, bring the narrative a poignant dimension of shared grief. These women, who had followed and supported Jesus, now witness his suffering and death. Their weeping is not just an expression of personal sorrow but reflects the communal impact of trauma. It underscores the way Jesus' suffering extends beyond his person to affect a wider circle of relationships.

> "The pain that death causes is . . . like a wound that cuts too deep to mend.
>
> "Sadness, anger, guilt, and confusion, all surge and overwhelm me. My mind is consumed by this intrusion. I am struggling to find my helm. Will it ever return?

"Days drag by, and nights are longer. Nothing at all brings any joy. My heart is scattered, my spirit is torn asunder, as I try to fight off the fear . . . Is it real? Is he truly gone?

"The pain of death manifests physically and emotionally. My strength is waning, my body is stressed. I am still trying to press through.

"Time and wounds—the things they say. Me? I'll take it as it comes; honoring the memories for my heart's sake and trying to find a new path and way.

"The pain of death will always be a reminder of the love we shared; of the impact my loved ones had on me; of the moments that we both cared." (Journal excerpt)

Mary's Pain

Mary is the mother of Jesus. She did not stand at the crucifixion with eyes closed in quiet contemplation. This was not a graduation ceremony, so she was not screaming his name in jubilation or anticipation of a bright future. The woman was in hell. Her grief was multiplied and was everywhere she turned. She was hyper-aware of the reality before her. This was not a horror movie that she could turn away her head from, walk away from, mute, or switch the channel. Her presence here is a study in trauma, encapsulating the depth of maternal grief and the piercing agony of witnessing the suffering and death of her child. She is remembering every word of Simeon's prophecy during the presentation of Jesus at the temple and how it foreshadows this pain, indicating that a sword would pierce Mary's own soul (Luke 2:35). If she were UMC, at his baptism, she would have vowed to reject the evil powers of this world, resist evil, injustice and oppression in whatever forms they presented themselves. Yet, here she stands, bent over, or rooting in the ground, witnessing an evil unlike any she had ever known, and powerless to prevent it or help her child.

The Trauma of Witnessing

At the crucifixion, Mary stands as a witness to the brutal execution of her own son. It hits different when this is your own womb giving testimony. This witnessing is characterized by horror. The visceral pain of watching her son, whom she carried, nurtured, and raised, being unjustly accused, tortured, and killed is absolutely unimaginable. Her trauma is not only emotional and psychological but also spiritual, as she grapples with the mystery of a suffering Messiah and the incomprehensible demands of what taunted her as divine providence. I am still stunned that she managed to survive. I think about how her body reacted to the sight of her son. What did her heartbeat do with every pounding of the nail? Personally, I have refused to romanticize any of this, because I have found it to be unhelpful.

I stand beside this mother, and my heart breaks with hers. My own maternal instinct just longs to comfort her, yet I find myself at a loss. So, I rock back and forth with her, letting the suppressed scream within me build momentum deep in my core. Crucifixion stings. So, I offer Mary my heartfelt groan. It is out of rhythm with hers, because you see, Jesus was not my son. I find that when I cry about this, my tears are especially salty because I cry not only for myself but also for her and the countless other mothers whose shared language is the raw, tearful form of expression that we know as weeping/hollering/bawling. If a woman had written the passion narrative, Mary would have received her day. Of course, it was written by those who don't have wombs, so they pressed mute on the sound of her pain. This is also not the kind of reading you share on a first date. This is a weird intersection that draws us in to explore how sometimes redemptive experiences can also be deeply wounding.

Mary's trauma at the crucifixion is a poignant reminder of the human cost of redemption. Her silent yet searing sorrow testifies to the complexities of grief, the realities of empathetic pain, and the enduring hope that, somehow, even in the worst moments, God is intimately present in our suffering. But it can be hard as hell to believe.

Chapter 74

Identifying a Theology That Addresses Trauma

So, A THEOLOGY THAT effectively addresses the experience of living in the aftermath of trauma is one that emphasizes God's presence in suffering, the redemptive power of shared experiences, and the hope of restoration. This perspective can be rooted in a "theology of accompaniment," which posits that God walks alongside individuals in their suffering, echoing the Christian belief in a God who experienced human pain and sorrow. It recognizes the incarnation and the passion of Christ not just as historical events but as ongoing realities in the lives of those who suffer.

This theology also leans on the concept of "lament," which is a vital but, sadly, an often underrepresented theme in the Christian tradition. As demonstrated by the Scriptures, we can give voice to the pain and confusion that accompany suffering, affirming that bringing our deepest hurts to God is a valid and necessary form of worship.

The Role of Community in Healing

As I immerse myself in thinking about Jesus' execution, I am once again drawn in by theologian Shelly Rambo's work in her book *Spirit and Trauma* and how she describes the need to hold the space between the horror and the hope. As we talked about the sense of abandonment that Jesus felt hanging there, can this sense of abandonment be redeemed? Asking for a friend.

These women, in their quiet but resolute care for Jesus, do not turn away from suffering or despair. In their commitment to Jesus in his most vulnerable moments, they demonstrate this capacity to hold space amid chaos and destruction. We call this community.

Though their actions did not directly bring about THE resurrection, they paved the way for new life. This echoes Elaine Scarry's observation in *The Body in Pain* that such care "repairs the ground for the return of the world itself."[1] In moments where life as we know it is unraveling, their kind of holding—firm, gentle, unwavering—creates a sanctuary for the birth of new possibilities. We need that future. The question before us is: What kind of future will we cultivate? Will it be one shaped by division or by collective healing and support?

In less visible ways, prayer, and contemplation, as Julian of Norwich showed centuries ago, can weave us together even in times of isolation. Shelly Rambo's recent reflections remind us that witnesses to the resurrection "refuse to be disconnected."[2] As I connect with the witness of these steadfast followers of Jesus, their example appeals to me not to be left in solitude. And now, more than ever, I work hard to resist disconnecting and disconnection.

In healing trauma, the role of the community is vital. A theology of communal healing underscores the belief that no one should deal with the aftermath of trauma alone. It is within the community that a person can find empathy, support, and a shared sense of understanding. This approach is exemplified in the early Christian communities, where believers were encouraged to "bear one another's burdens" (Gal 6:2).

The concept of "shared witnessing" is crucial here, where the community not only listens to the stories of those who have suffered but also stands in solidarity with them. This act of witnessing

---

1. Scarry, *Body in Pain*, 34.
2. Rambo, "Hell of Holy Saturday."

is both healing and empowering. It validates the experiences of the traumatized and helps dismantle the isolation that often accompanies trauma.

Chapter 75

I Keep Returning to These Passages

"I can't explain. There may not be an explanation. I had a snotty-nosed, snotty-nosed meltdown today. Then I ate chocolate after chocolate, and now, my belly hurts like hell in so many ways.

"I went in the office this morning, and my desk had these beautiful handcrafted little paper bags with bookmarks and cards for me and the family from the youth director, Heather. That was such a good breath! This moment, I breathed.

"Then, later the preschool director was in the office. 'Hi Monique.' I greeted her. 'I love you, and we want you here,' she replied. I had a meltdown. Just like that . . . She waited, then asked to see a picture of Arleigh . . . 'O my God, Pastor, he was so handsome!' she exclaimed. 'Yes,' I said. 'Yes.' And I wept some more. I came back to the parsonage this afternoon, and Arleigha was having a meltdown of her own. She misses her brother.

"Where can we go to hide from this pain? It's consuming. I'm not so numb anymore, so I'm really feeling it. The hyper-awareness is killing me. I feel lost . . . so lost . . ." (Journal excerpt)

Psalm 137—Of Bashing Babies et al.

Reclaiming Grief and Trauma in the Church:
The Lessons of Ruth and Psalm 137

IN WRITING THIS BOOK, I found out that many people carry deep grief, yet they are often discouraged from bringing it to church. Many individuals face their own rivers of Babylon, as described in Ps 137, harboring imprecatory prayers buried deep within their hearts. It saddened me to learn that some have even forgotten Zion—losing the memory of joy and safety, which only compounds their trauma. Some have become hardened and embittered, while others, like my grandmother, openly weep for the first time. It is too easy to forget Zion and any semblance of a safe space if the church continues to misuse the Scriptures and fails to take better care of its wounded.

I spoke with a deeply churched Caribbean woman who was relieved that her government was finally addressing mental health. Although the need for such conversations and actions was evident, both the church and society had been waiting for the government to take the lead. This is distressing because the Christian church, which has long upheld the Bible, has largely ignored the numerous instances where trauma demands to be addressed. The church has abdicated its responsibility. While I am not a political analyst, I firmly believe that it is the church, not the government, that is first charged with bearing one another's burdens.

I have also encountered many stories of border crossing, as seen in the book of Ruth. Unfortunately, many of these encounters with supposed Boaz figures turned out disturbing. There were stories of forced and attempted forced sexual encounters, which people are still struggling with, too ashamed to speak of. The evidence of trauma is nonetheless present in their lives and relationships. Some of these individuals drive everyone around them to the brink as they try to control everything and everyone, projecting their insecurities onto others. I place some of this responsibility on the church for telling people to leave their troubles elsewhere when they gather for worship. How can a person leave their troubles behind? What happens after they leave the gathering? Where did this nonsense originate? Is God afraid of troubles? Once again, we make God comfortable only with what we are comfortable with. I need a God who is not scared or uncomfortable with my troubles. A lesser God is too shallow for my very deep life.

Although my mother only physically left the island once, she shared stories of her own border crossings with me. While working as a maid in Antigua, she was often harassed by the so-called men of the houses in which she worked. Her joy was immense when she got a job at the airport, eliminating one of her greatest fears. Hence, I posit that border crossings are not only the spaces that divide national and geographic territories.

My own border crossing could have been a much sadder account. I was propositioned in multiple ways by men inside and outside the church community, who saw me as prey—a woman with children but no man. They learned soon enough that they were messing with the wrong one! Unfortunately, not every woman who faced this kind of danger experienced a similar outcome.

Some of the border-crossing terrors shared by the women I spoke with were rooted in the US immigration system. Some were undocumented, and others, though documented, were still afraid of losing their statuses. The men who perpetrated the abuses were not always US nationals; some were immigrants themselves. This highlights how pervasive patriarchy is—men, regardless of their immigration status, still felt empowered to overpower women. How dangerous this is! National men would threaten to report the women for being in the US "illegally." The awful reality is that we live in a world that often profits from violence against immigrants. Belittling and dehumanizing someone should never be part of any conversation around structural construction. Such inhumane behaviors often promote a morphogenesis of the self, spiraling downward into self-abasement. As I reflect on these stories, it becomes clear how rare Ruth's kind of romantic outcome is. Zion can easily disappear in the face of dangers such as what should be simple border crossings.

Chapter 76

Remembering Zion

ZION IS ALSO A many-splendored thing. After Arleigh died, my cousin and her family came and stayed in the first days. She was driving back and forth for close to an hour every few days to stay with us. My clergy covenant sisters showed up to be with me. They slept on my couches and their help and presence became balm. Along with other clergy colleagues, they showed up and sat with my family, cleaned our bathrooms, swept the floor, kept us company, chatted nonsense, and drove my children back and forth. One clergy sister came by and cleaned and when she noticed that I was having a meltdown, she sat with me. None of them ran when I cried. Friends came and cooked, cleaned, watered my plants, and played live music for me. Arleigh's friends came and regaled us with stories that he used to regale them with. Did I tell you: he was a comedian who would have you howling with laughter until tears ran down your legs! We got letters from his students and notes from out-of-town friends. Clergy brothers came by and stayed a while, holding me with their care. In those moments, I remembered and re-membered Zion.

I showed Arleigh's friends his baby album. He would have been mortified! Or maybe he would have gloated. He was a cute, cute, cute baby, who grew into a very handsome young man! The preschool director and youth director at Epworth UMC, whom I met less than a year after Arleigh's death, made pushing through the thirty-five-minute traffic, alone with my pain to get to my new workspace among strangers, during a pandemic, all worthwhile. They were kind. People are at their most vulnerable when grieving, and the people who showed up without the need for fanfare understood that compassion, like generosity is a core element of Christianity. Zion showed up in inane objects like the music I love—calypso, soca, and reggae. I also remembered Zion in people who were disconnected from the church, whose emotional intelligence was a gift to my family. None of these expected a return on their investment of the time spent with me.

There is something unnamed and painful about the pressure to respond in a prescribed manner that is more about other people's capacity, than about the person who is in pain. Thus, too many people do not have a good church support system in their hours of despair. Despair is messy, and all too damn real.

Despair by any other name is still despair and it often does not know the way out. "Did you lose your faith?" "We want back our pastor." "The boy is with God. You should know better and stop behaving so." "Are you worried about where your son is?" Oh! And the classic shit: "Her tears are not genuine." What the words-the-pastor-should-not-print-unless-she-is-fighting-off-demons? Seriously? I have some questions of my own: What happened to *your* soul? Have *you* lost *your* soul? Was it your womb that carried *my* child? What real contribution did you make to his life that you feel entitled to question the weight of *my* grief?

I find the kind of ignorance that comes out of one human being to another to be malignant. It is born out of a lack of proper, emotionally intelligent engagement with life. It is nurtured in the womb of hearsay from an onlooker's perch, often fed by gossip and a desire to hide one's own pain behind the skewed examination of someone else's. It is both a bully and a coward.

"You need to find your faith again." This said, as if faith is about proving the existence of God. As if faith does not exist in the same space with despair, trauma, and life's uncertainties. Would we also accuse Jesus of needing to find his faith again when we encounter him in the record of his bleakest moments? There really are not sufficient words that can communicate this extraordinary thing called grief that is so deeply embedded in ordinary life. It is dislocating, tenacious, unrelenting, and tethered to the things that undo life. Yet, confronting it is connected to liberation and is a viable source of healing and relocation.

Part 3

Reflection and Guidance

Some Journal Entries

2019

10.02

Why the hell is time moving in the direction that it is? Doesn't time know that it should be moving backwards? Does it not know that I have a child to warn and keep alive? What the hell is wrong with time?

Time does its own dam thing

As if it has no master

It's moving faster, faster, and faster

To a beat

That doesn't meet

The expectations of my heart.

In a swift run of time's movement,

Life shifted.

Time, they say, heals all wounds.

I'm wounded. I keep feeling wounded because time won't move backwards.

What the hell is wrong with time? Does it not know that I have a child to warn and keep alive?

10.04

The days run as the nights do: empty, except for the pain. I do not like this place where I find myself. I'm told that God is with me and always has been. It's disconcerting to learn that the God whom I have always loved and espoused is the God who has released me into this seriously challenging place in my life.

I'm concerned about my other children. I do not think that they are processing this harsh reality. I'm worried about me. I do not want to let them out of my sight. I cannot pray—for myself or for them. I want to pray. I just cannot. I am disoriented and feel dislocated, completely lost.

10.16

There is no training for this. No way to prepare. No warning about what to avoid.

Mrs. Job, can I speak to you? I understand your distrust, your woundedness, your sorrow. I cannot know for sure its depth as I am not you. I do know that I lament with you out of another dark place of losing a part of myself.

Arleigh is my son, whom I carried, prayed for, and raised and still love deeply. My womb hurts. It throbs spontaneously as if getting ready to give birth. Mrs. Job, did this happen to you too? Did you too feel the cold darkness resting on your belly and tugging at your breast as if to taunt you? Mrs. Job, how did you manage?

11.10

My family is no longer whole. My family has a hole. Arleigh is missing. My child . . .

PART 3: REFLECTION AND GUIDANCE

2020

05.10

I feel scattered and betrayed. Today is celebrated as Mother's Day. I feel destroyed because although I have the other three children here, I hurt so bad because of Arleigh's death. I still don't get it. I don't even know what it is that I "don't get."

06.28

Today is Sunday. The last Sunday in June. July is quickly approaching. It will be August 24th soon. What will I do, God? What will I do?

06.30

Soca. I played soca all day today. I danced until my knees begged me to stop. I did not listen to them because my heart felt slightly less tensioned by the activity.

07.06

Today, I'm remembering stooping on the shoreline of the Sea of Galilee, Israel. I remember feeling anxious, raw, and emotionally depleted. I remember the cry of my heart. Since then, besides the time, a few things have changed: I am more protective of my heart and my children. I am more self-aware and recognize my triggers more easily. I am more patient and gentler with myself (most days). I seek no one's permission to embrace my emotions. I make no apology for mourning my child's death.

Many other things remain unshaken: I still love my children fiercely; love my husband fiercely; believe in God's call on my life; abhor and resist evil, injustice, and oppression in whatever forms they present themselves (read systemic racism, systemic racism, systemic racism, hypocrisy, xenophobia, homophobia, et al.). I am still a pescatarian; enjoy being creative, making soap and gardening; love the gift and art of prophetic preaching; love (singing + dancing to) calypso and soca; love Bob Marley + Peter Tosh; love playing the steel pan; scared of gossips, frogs, and dogs.

Much has remained the same. Much has changed. I have remained the same. I have been forever changed.

Life.

07.07

I miss Arleigh. My heart feels squeezed by the hurt that presses in on it. I talked to him today, and his initial silence was painful. Then the next thing I knew, he was there making me laugh.

08.14

My belly!!! I miss my child. Arleigh!!! Why??? O Gawwwd!!!

08.21

I can't push back the anxiety that's on me. It's a few days short of a year since Arleigh became part of the heavenly host. I miss him so much. I hurt so badly. So badly . . .

08.24

Did this day need to arrive? Why can't we go back to a time before I can stop Arleigh from riding? Why is my child dead? Why is my family in so much pain? Why can't we change events??? It's a year. A whole year since the police came and delivered the heart-breaking shitty news that my Arleigh has died. One whole year. My child!! I feel like shit! O God! I prayed for my children's safety, every f_cking day! And You let this shit happen! I want my child!!!

2022

08.13

Isaiah 42:14: "For a long time I have held my peace, I have kept still and restrained myself; now I will cry out like a woman in labor, I will gasp and pant."

I've given birth to four children without the aid of medicine. The labors didn't last any more than a few hours and even less than two hours on three occasions, although the pregnancies were horrible. The pain of giving birth is unlike any other. I have difficulty describing it. Although I have never screamed during labor, I gasped and panted, and I have heard other women in neighboring rooms let out blood-curdling sounds while they were in labor.

When the police came and informed me of my son's death, I felt that pain again—even more searing than it did in the summer of 1995 when I gave birth to him. This time, I could not keep silent. The sound made its way from the soles of my feet, sat for a bit in my womb, then rushed out as if seeking oxygen. It found oxygen because it continues to live. It lives at the slightest provocation and sometimes no visible provocation at all. It calls back to my mind the panting of the moment. Therapy has introduced different breathing methods to help me cope with the rush of physical pain. Isaiah's panting God reminds me of the creation story where it is said that God breathed the breath of life into the first human and that human became a living being (Gen 2:7). Breath is life.

Conclusion

LAMENT IS AN IMPORTANT aspect of the Christian faith that has been present since ancient times. It is a form of prayer that expresses sorrow, pain, and grief in response to suffering and loss. Lament acknowledges the reality of human brokenness and the need for God's comfort and mercy in times of distress.

The value of lament can be seen in several biblical accounts, including the book of Psalms, the book of Lamentations, and the book of Job. In these books, we see individuals pouring out their hearts to God, expressing their pain and confusion, and seeking comfort and hope in the midst of their suffering.

Lament is a way of connecting with God and with one another in a deep and meaningful way. It allows us to be vulnerable and honest about our emotions, even when they are difficult to express. Lament also helps us to recognize the suffering of others and to respond with empathy and compassion.

Furthermore, lament reminds us that we are not alone in our suffering. God is present with us, and we can trust in his love and faithfulness, even in the darkest of times. Lament helps us to remember that our hope is not in ourselves or in our circumstances, but in the grace and mercy of God.

The value of lament lies in its ability to bring us closer to God and to one another, to express our emotions honestly, and to find comfort and hope in the midst of our suffering. As we engage in lament, we are reminded of God's love and faithfulness, and we are strengthened to face the challenges of life with courage and resilience.

The church must rediscover its identity as a sanctuary for the wounded—a place where lament is not only allowed but also honored as an integral part of faith. This work demands a shift from theologies that rush to resolution and platitudes, to practices that make space for pain, uncertainty, and the slow work of healing. Walking alongside those dealing with personal or communal trauma requires intentionality, creativity, and courage. Below are practical steps for pastors and congregations to embody the work of solidarity, healing, and justice.

1. Naming the Traumas

The church cannot walk alongside the traumatized if it does not first name the pain. Traumas—whether personal, communal, or systemic—must be acknowledged openly in worship and pastoral care. Silence, when it comes to trauma, often exacerbates pain and alienation. By naming these realities, the church affirms the humanity of those who suffer and disrupts the tendency to minimize or ignore their stories.

Contextualized Ceremonies

Blue Christmas Services

Host services during Advent that acknowledge grief, loss, and longing. Use Scripture, poetry, and music that resonate with the weight of pain many carry into the holiday season. Avoid clichés and focus on creating sacred space for mourning and reflection.

Services of Remembrance

Create opportunities throughout the year to commemorate communal traumas. This might include anniversaries of natural disasters, moments of racial reckoning, or events like September 11. Rituals such as lighting candles, naming victims, and communal prayers of lament can offer solidarity and healing.

Trauma Sundays

Designate a Sunday to reflect on traumas in the community, including those stemming from systemic oppression. Offer sermons and liturgies that connect the experiences of the people to biblical stories of lament, justice, and renewal.

Easter and Trauma

Easter celebrations should resist the tendency to center overly simplistic atonement theologies while ignoring the historical and systemic sin that crucified Jesus. Highlight the trauma of Jesus' arrest, trial, and crucifixion as the result of humanity's failure to build equitable systems of justice. Preach about the complicity of empire, the abandonment of the disciples, and the public spectacle of violence, situating these events in the larger narrative of human suffering and divine solidarity. This framing makes space for survivors to find themselves in the story without feeling blamed or excluded.

2. *Integrating Lament into Worship*

Lament must be reclaimed as a central act of Christian worship. Far from being an obstacle to praise, lament is a profound expression of faith that acknowledges both the reality of pain and the hope for transformation.

Portable Wailing Wall

Borrowing from the imagery of the Western Wall in Jerusalem, create a "wailing wall" in the sanctuary or through liturgical practice. This could be a physical structure where congregants can write prayers, laments, and petitions to place in its crevices. Alternatively, incorporate a "wall" into the liturgy, allowing space for people to name their grief aloud or silently during the service. I have created multiple wailing walls using various devices.

Prayers of the People

Revise traditional prayers of intercession to include specific, contextual laments. For example:

> "For those grieving loved ones lost to violence, neglect, and systemic oppression, we cry out: God, hear our prayer."

> "For communities displaced by war, economic injustice, or natural disasters, we cry out: God, hear our prayer."

These prayers should reflect the congregation's lived reality and affirm that God is present in the midst of suffering.

The Art of Silence

Incorporate intentional moments of silence into the liturgy to allow space for personal reflection and the unspeakable groans of the heart (Rom 8:26). Silence can be a powerful container for communal grief and solidarity.

3. Preaching from the Margins

Pastoral preaching must acknowledge and engage the pain present in the congregation and the world. Sermons should:

Center Marginalized Voices

Draw connections between biblical narratives and the lived experiences of those who suffer today. Preach the stories of Tamar, Job, Hagar, and the prophets not as distant moral lessons but as mirrors of the congregation's struggles.

Resist Simplistic Solutions

Avoid platitudes like "God has a plan" or "Everything happens for a reason." Instead, affirm the complexity of suffering and the reality of unanswered questions, while pointing to God's steadfast presence.

Elevate Communal Responsibility

Challenge the congregation to address systemic trauma through advocacy, justice work, and communal care. Preach a vision of faith that integrates lament with action.

4. Pastoral Care for Trauma Survivors

Walking alongside individuals who have experienced trauma requires sensitivity, training, and a commitment to avoid retraumatization.

Active Listening

Pastors should prioritize being present over providing answers. Listen without rushing to fix or theologize the pain. Trauma survivors often need to be heard, not instructed.

Avoiding Spiritual Bypass

Do not minimize pain by over-spiritualizing it. For example, avoid statements like "God never gives us more than we can handle." Instead, validate the survivor's feelings and affirm their courage in the face of suffering.

Collaborating with Professionals

Pastors can offer counsel, but are not generally therapists, though some are specifically trained thus. However, they can collaborate with trauma-informed counselors to provide holistic care. Keep a list of vetted professionals to whom congregants can be referred.

Training Lay Leaders

Equip lay leaders with basic training in trauma-informed care. These leaders can help extend the church's pastoral reach while ensuring survivors receive the care they need.

PART 3: REFLECTION AND GUIDANCE

5. Communal Practices of Healing

Trauma is not only personal but also communal. The church must create spaces where the entire body (and bodies) can engage in practices of collective healing.

Art and Creativity

Introduce communal art projects, such as creating a quilt, mosaic, or mural that reflects the congregation's journey through trauma. These projects can be sacred acts of remembrance and hope.

Pilgrimages

Organize pilgrimages to places of historical or communal significance, such as visiting sites of racial injustice, environmental degradation, or cultural heritage. These journeys can be opportunities for reflection, education, and solidarity.

Communal Fast and Feast

Invite the congregation to participate in a day of fasting to mourn specific traumas, followed by a communal meal that symbolizes hope and restoration. If the trauma has no utility for healing, then contextualize to suit. Perhaps, the type of meal—bread and water—is sufficient a demonstration.

6. Embodying Justice

Healing requires addressing the root causes of trauma. The church must actively work to dismantle systems of oppression and build equitable communities.

Advocacy

Organize campaigns to address systemic issues such as racial injustice, economic inequality, and gender-based violence. Partner with local organizations and amplify the voices of those most affected.

Educational Opportunities

Host workshops and Bible studies that explore the intersections of faith, justice, and trauma. Provide tools for congregants to understand and address systemic harms.

Community Partnerships

Collaborate with secular organizations, mental health professionals, and community leaders to expand the church's capacity to respond to trauma.

For Further Thinking

General

>Why do people create excuses for God when bad things happen?
>
>Why are we afraid to ask God questions?
>
>Why are we so afraid to own up to our uncertainties?
>
>What are the implications of our pretenses?
>
>How do you feel when you hear that there is trauma in the Bible?
>
>How do you hear stories such as Bathsheba's and the plight of the marginalized in light of Isaiah 59:14–16?

Psalm 137

>How do we reconcile the love of Christ with the action of blessing those who take the babies of our enemies and dash their heads against rocks?
>
>How can these verses be interpreted in our time and contexts?
>
>Imagine you are the Babylonians. How do you hear this text? Now imagine you are the ones being oppressed; how do you hear this text?

Name at least one Babylon that you have experienced.

What or who represents Zion for you? (Name as many as you can.)

How do you remember Zion?

Ruth

Where do you locate yourself in the foregoing?

How does your location in the book of Ruth make you feel?

How have you used any agency that you have to either harm or heal?

Job

Imagine you are visiting Mrs. Job after the announcement of the first child's death. What would your visit look like?

If you have or haven't visited the Job family after the first child's death, by the fifth child's death, where are you?

What is your immediate emotional response to Mrs. Job's reported advice to Mr. Job?

"Shall we receive good from God and not bad?" Why do we have the construct of the problem of unexplained suffering, and we don't have the problem of unexplained blessing?

Can we serve God when things are not going well as we serve God when things are going well?

Given the backdrop of the deaths of children and the insidious evil of racism, which manifests in the dismissal and dehumanization of people of color, how do we reconcile these harsh realities with the church's proclamation of God's goodness?

A Letter to the Grieving

GRIEF IS NOT A detour. Grief is the path. In the words of my Granny and the people of her era, "It's a road for all of us." Grief twists and turns, takes us to valleys we never wished to tread, and leads us to summits from which we glimpse the beauty of what we have lost. It is not linear, nor is it predictable, but it is sacred. Every tear shed and every lament uttered becomes an offering at the altar of our pain as a witness to the depth of love we have known.

To grieve is to remember that love cannot be extinguished by death. It lingers in the echoes of laughter, in the scent of familiar places, in the way we still set the table for one more, even when we know they won't physically come. Grief is not a betrayal of faith; it is an act of faith. To mourn is to trust that God meets us in the bleakness, not so much to snatch us away from it, but to walk with us through it.

Through the pages of this book, I have shared some of my own journey as a companion. It is not a road map. I have laid bare some of my struggles, questions, anger, and hope. I have called out the ways the church has failed in its duty to hold those who grieve, and I have called in the church to a vision for a community that does better. It is a community that sits in the ashes with those who mourn, that acknowledges the unbearable weight of loss without rushing to fix it, that allows lament to rise as an act of worship, holy and raw.

If you find yourself in the depths of grief, whether you are mourning the death of a loved one, or other personal and communal trauma, know this: you are not broken. You are not lost. You are not failing. You are navigating one of the hardest and most sacred human experiences. Allow yourself to feel it all—including moments of laughter that surprise you. Allow yourself to weep, to rage, to question. And know that God is present in all your moments, not as an answer to be found but as a presence to be felt.

And to the church, as you walk alongside the grieving, and as you, too, grieve: Be still. Be present. Be willing to stand in the tension of what cannot be fixed. Honor the tears of the bereaved as holy water and their cries as sacred songs. Be willing to cry your own tears. Grief is not a problem to be solved but a truth to be witnessed. In our witnessing, we make space for healing by honoring its depth and allowing hope to grow alongside it.

This is my prayer for you, dear reader: that you may walk this path of lament with courage, that you may find companions who honor your journey, and that you may find, in the mystery of it all, a God who weeps with us and yet promises that one day, all tears will be wiped away. Until that day, may we lament boldly, love deeply, and live fully.

Holding space for you,

Andrea

Tips for the Lament Journey

- Commit to your own education and process
- It is okay to tell God where it hurts
- Own your trauma
- Do not allow anyone to design your grief
- Write your own lament
- Remember what you cannot forget
- Remember that God prefers our authentic angst to our pretentious praise

For Further Reading

- *Reading the Bible from the Margins* by Miguel De La Torre
- *Other Ways of Reading* by Musa Dube
- *Yet with a Steady Beat* edited by Randall Bailey
- *Womanist Midrash* by Wil Gafney
- *The Africana Bible* edited by Hugh R. Page Jr.
- "A Long Ways from Home: Displacement, Lament, and Singing Protest in Psalm 137" by Valerie Bridgeman. A version of this article was presented in the Project Psalms Section at the XXII Congress of the International Organization for the Study of the Old Testament, 4–9 September 2016, Stellenbosch, South Africa.

Bibliography

Bonhoeffer, Dietrich. *A Testament to Freedom: The Essential Writings of Dietrich Bonhoeffer*. Edited by Geffrey B. Kelly and F. Burton Nelson. San Francisco: HarperOne, 2009.
Brown, Francis, et al. *A Hebrew and English Lexicon of the Old Testament*. Peabody, MA: Hendrickson, 1994.
Carter, Warren. *Mark*. Wisdom Commentary 42. Collegeville, MN: Liturgical, 2020.
Fallon, Michael. *The Gospel According to St Luke*. Kensington, NSW: Chevalier, 2007.
Fentress-Williams, Judy. *Ruth*. Nashville: Abingdon, 2012.
Gafney, Wilda C. *Womanist Midrash*. Vol. 1, *A Reintroduction to the Women of the Torah and the Throne*. Louisville, KY: Westminster John Knox, 2017.
———. *A Women's Lectionary for the Whole Church, Year W*. New York: Church Publishing, 2021.
Goldingay, John. *Psalms*. Vol. 1, *Psalm 1–41*. Baker Commentary on the Old Testament Wisdom and Psalms. Grand Rapids: Baker Academic, 2006.
Gutiérrez, Gustavo. *On Job: God-Talk and the Suffering of the Innocent*. New York: Orbis, 1987.
Havea, Jione, and Peter H. W. Lau. *Reading Ruth in Asia*. Atlanta: SBL, 2015.
The Hymnal of The Evangelical United Brethren Church. Dayton, OH: The Evangelical United Brethren Church, 1957.
Krisel, William. "Was the Levite's Concubine Unfaithful or Angry? A Proposed Solution to the Text Critical Problem in Judges 19:2." 2020. https://www.academia.edu/44941459/Was_the_levites_concubine_unfaithful_or_angry_a_prosed_solution_to_the_text_critical_problem_in_judges_19_2.
Murrell, Nathaniel Samuel, et al. "Psalms." In *The African Bible: Reading Israel's Scriptures from Africa and the African Diaspora*, edited by Hugh R. Page Jr. Minneapolis: Fortress, 2010.
Nieuwhof, Carey. "Rick Warren on Finishing Well." YouTube video, Jan. 4, 2022. https://www.youtube.com/watch?v=X03gY7HPr7Q.

Berlin, Adele, ed. *The Oxford Dictionary of the Jewish Religion*. 2nd ed. Oxford University Press, 2011.

Rambo, Shelly. "The Hell of Holy Saturday." *The Christian Century*, Apr. 7, 2020. https://www.christiancentury.org/blog-post/guest-post/hell-holy-saturday.

———. *Spirit and Trauma: A Theology of Remaining*. Louisville, KY: Westminster John Knox, 2010.

Reagan, Ronald. "Farewell Address to the Nation." Ronald Reagan Presidential Library and Museum, Jan. 11, 1989. https://www.reaganlibrary.gov/archives/speech/farewell-address-nation.

Rosenbloom, Deborah. "Op-Ed: Rethinking the Ruth-Naomi Relationship." *STL Jewish Light*, May 7, 2013. https://stljewishlight.org/news/world-news/op-ed-rethinking-the-ruth-naomi-relationship/.

Sanders, Cheryl J. "African American Worship in the Pentecostal and Holiness Movements." *Wesleyan Theological Journal* 32.2 (Fall 1997) 105–20.

———. *Saints in Exile: The Holiness-Pentecostal Experience in African American Religion and Culture*. Oxford: Oxford University Press, 1996.

Scarry, Elaine. *The Body in Pain*. Oxford: Oxford University Press, 1987.

Shipp, R. Mark. "How Can We Sing the Lord's Song? The Psalms as the Church's Hymnal." Lectureship and Summit Audio Collection, Sept. 23, 2009. https://digitalcommons.acu.edu/sumlec_audio/771.

Strong, James. *The New Strong's Exhaustive Concordance of the Bible*. Nashville: Thomas Nelson, 1995.

Van der Kolk, Bessel. *The Body Keeps the Score: Brain, Mind and Body in the Healing of Trauma*. New York: Penguin, 2015.

Wink, Walter. *Engaging the Powers: Discernment and Resistance in a World of Domination*. Minneapolis: Fortress, 1992.

www.ingramcontent.com/pod-product-compliance
Lightning Source LLC
Chambersburg PA
CBHW071228170426
43191CB00032B/1127